GILBERT AND SULLIVAN

HESKETH PEARSON

GILBERT AND
SULLIVAN

A Biography

Introduction by Malcolm Muggeridge

MACDONALD AND JANE'S · LONDON

To Madge and Colin Hurry

First published in Great Britain by
Hamish Hamilton Ltd. in 1935

Reissued in 1975 by
Macdonald and Jane's,
Macdonald and Company (Publishers) Ltd.,
Paulton House,
8 Shepherdess Walk,
London N1

ISBN 0 356 08034 X

Printed in Great Britain by
REDWOOD BURN LIMITED
Trowbridge & Esher

CONTENTS

LIST OF ILLUSTRATIONS

INTRODUCTION

In writing this Introduction, it is a great satisfaction to me to have an opportunity of recalling the many hours of delightful companionship I spent with Hesketh Pearson, whose death, in April 1964, so impoverished his friends, myself among them. When I think of him, of his qualities, gifts and a special gusto which characterized everything he said and did and was, what I most vividly recall is the accompanying laughter. His favourite response to life was to laugh, and it was impossible to be with him for long without catching the infection. Striding along London streets or over Hampstead Heath – a favourite occupation – riding on the tops of buses, seated in pubs or cafés or in one another's homes, whatever subject cropped up, laughter would never be far away. In his company, even politics turned out to be funny, and as for religion – as in his estimation there was only one worthy of serious consideration, and that embodied in the doctrine, liturgy and episcopal establishment of the Church of England in which he had been brought up, with a large supporting cast of clerical forbears, discussion of it, too, tended to be conducted in a light-hearted vein. The fact is that there was a parson lurking somewhere in

Hesketh's make-up; it was not by chance that his first successful book was *The Smith of Smiths*, a biography of Sidney Smith, the famous eighteenth-century clergyman and wit. His own voice had a decidedly clerical ring about it, and in repose he was liable to press his fingers together and wear an expression of studied amiability in true parsonical style.

My first meeting with Hesketh was, as it were, *in absentia*, on Stockport railway station on a dreary, rainy afternoon in the autumn of 1930. I was working on the *Manchester Guardian* (as it then was), and Hugh Kingsmill, who was spending the weekend with me, had somehow got it into his head that his friend Hesketh Pearson would be passing through Stockport on his way south on the Sunday afternoon. At that time Hesketh was earning his living on the stage, and touring with a repertory company. The only two parts that I can remember his specifically mentioning were the junior lead in *The Matriarch*, an undistinguished play whose London production was glorified by the presence of Mrs Patrick Campbell in the title role, and the heroine's father in De Vere Stackpool's *The Blue Lagoon*. The great advantage of the latter part was that, as the ship on which the heroine's father was travelling was wrecked at the end of the first act, leaving his daughter and a putative mate to clamber ashore on a nearby desert island where the remaining action of the play took place, Hesketh had nothing to do for the rest of the performance except hang around for the final curtain. He loved to describe how, after playing the part for two years in an access of boredom he carelessly put on his head a large panama hat he had been given by the props man to carry in his hand, only to find that it was several sizes too small. The effect on the audience was electric, and momentarily stopped the show. Among his friends, the general opinion was that Hesketh's acting was spirited rather than star-quality, but he continued to love the theatre to the end of his days, and his reminiscences of it, and mimicry of eminent figures in it like Beerbohm Tree and Frank Benson, were a delight to one and all. Also, as readers of this volume will soon discover, he was an ardent addict of Gilbert and Sullivan light opera, and fascinated by a partnership which proved so superbly successful professionally, and yet was so troubled and discordant personally.

While Kingsmill and I waited for Hesketh's hypothetical arrival at Stockport Station, we walked up and down the bleak platform talking incessantly. It was the first time I realised how utterly captivating Kingsmill's conversation could be, and thenceforth came to prize it as one of life's major alleviations. I scarcely noticed the passage of time, or the drab surroundings, or the dismal weather, for the fascination of our talk; and even now, looking back across more than forty years, it seems as though Stockport Station must be a delectable spot, on a par with, say, the Bay of Naples. Hesketh never did show up. Nor was there, as I subsequently discovered, the faintest reason to suppose that he would, or, for that matter, any train due that afternoon which could possibly have brought him from wherever he was. Nonetheless, so vivid was Kingsmill's account of him that it seemed as though we had actually met, and when some five years later I made his acquaintance in the flesh, it was as an already established friend.

Thereafter, the three of us were together often, and it became a firm and steady triple friendship, with Kingsmill in the centre, and Hesketh and myself on the two flanks, and in a certain sense, communicating through him. I have long considered friendship to be the nearest to a totally disinterested relationship which we humans can achieve, and therefore one of our special blessings. Certainly, this particular friendship proved so for me. How clearly I can recall, as I write these words, the walks we took, the books we interminably discussed, the scenes we reconstructed, the games we played – as: If we had an opportunity to spend an evening with two great literary figures from the past, which would we choose? Kingsmill usually plumped for Dr Johnson whom he revered, and Wordsworth whom he considered the greatest English poet, and Hesketh for Shakespeare out of a passionate loyalty to the Bard and all his works, and Wilde for the delight of his conversation. My own choice was for Swift and

Blake. I was the youngest of the three, and am now the only survivor – a reflection which reminds me of how Hesketh, basically a very emotional person, much more so than appeared on first acquaintance, never could manage to complete Wordsworth's lines on the Death of James Hogg without breaking down:

> How fast has brother followed brother,
> From sunshine to the sunless land.

Both Hesketh and I got much more, in terms of ideas and insights, out of Kingsmill than he from us. He was our Master, and when we were alone together more often than not we talked about him or echoed him. The fact that he nonetheless found it so much harder to earn a living with his pen than we did struck us as unfair, and we tried – especially Hesketh – to correct matters by seizing every opportunity that offered to acknowledge our debt to him and his pre-eminence as a literary critic. After a false start with his *The Whispering Gallery*, amusingly described in his autobiography *Hesketh Pearson By Himself*, Hesketh got going with *The Smith of Smiths*, and with his Shaw and Wilde biographies became, if not exactly a best-seller – whatever that may mean – a highly successful writer who could count upon a substantial readership for whatever he chose to write.

There was never any question but that biography was his field. Most writers who excel in one *genre* aspire after others, like Henry James wanting to write successful plays, or Thomas Hardy wanting to write a great epic poem. Hesketh never deviated in his passion for biographical writing, which satisfied his enormous curiosity about his fellow-humans and enabled him to indulge his love of anecdotage. To him, literature was people rather than situations or ideas; when he was writing his book on Shaw he found it extremely difficult to persuade himself that so witty and accomplished a dramatist could possibly be seriously interested in politics. As for exploring the origins of Shaw's political view – for Hesketh, it would have been like exploring the theological implications of St Francis's Canticle of the Sun. The fact that Shaw had undoubtedly been influenced by Karl Marx no more induced him to plough his way through *Das Kapital* than writing a biography of his ancestor Erasmus Darwin induced him to tackle seriously the works of Erasmus's grandson, Charles. While he was working on the Shaw book I took Hesketh to see the Webbs, they being – especially Sidney – Shaw's political mentors. In the event, the conversation turned almost exclusively on Frank Harris, of whom Sidney Webb had memories, which, however, as he had recently suffered a stroke, he had great difficulty in conveying. All we could make of his ejaculations sounded like 'a bull-dog round your neck'. Meditating upon this enigmatic phrase afterwards, we decided it perhaps related to Harris's sense of what being married to a rich woman was like, and carried the implication that Webb found himself in a similar case. This, we considered, may have accounted for the indignation with which Webb appeared to look back on the experience of lunching with Harris in his Park Lane days of affluence-by-marriage.

Hesketh's method as a biographer was to get inside his subject's skin rather than into his mind or even his soul. To do this he needed to find his subject essentially sympathetic. Certainly, he could never have tackled anyone he positively disliked. His affection for his subjects, as for his friends, led him to be leniently disposed towards their faults and tolerant of their misdemeanours. Thus, as he intensely disliked any form of sexual perversion and yet held Oscar Wilde in great affection and admiration, he was inclined to pooh pooh the, alas, all too well established charges of perverse practices at Wilde's trial. In *The Fool of Love*, too – an excellent book – he leans over backwards to present the *Liber Amoris* affair in a way which reflects the least discredit on Hazlitt. The truth is that the subjects of Hesketh's biographies became a circle of absent friends whom he felt bound to champion in all circumstances and on all counts. One of the few occasions on which we exchanged angry words arose out of a review I wrote of his book on Tom Paine, to whom I referred as having become at the end of his life a garrulous drunken bum. Hesketh took great exception to this, but as always happened with him, his anger soon evaporated, and he perhaps saw that

I had a point. Despite occasional explosions of rage, he had a singularly sweet disposition, incapable of nursing a grievance or harbouring resentment against a friend, and benevolently disposed towards animals and men, in that order.

It would be quite wrong to suppose that, because Hesketh's attitude to the subjects of his biographies was so personal, and at times idiosyncratic, they lack verisimilitude. On the contrary, affection and admiration are by and large truer guides than hostility and denigration. After all, the greatest biographies in the English language, like Boswell's Johnson, Mrs Gaskel's Charlotte Brontë and Carlyle's John Sterling, are affectionate and respectful, and already the waspish facetiousness of a Lytton Strachey has become outmoded and largely forgotten. Like many of his generation Hesketh began by wholeheartedly admiring *Eminent Victorians* as a pleasant relief from the unction and sycophancy of Victorian biography, but he was temperamentally incapable of emulating Strachey's waspish approach even if he had wanted to. The portrait gallery of biographical studies he left behind him is as different from Strachey's as is a glass of draught ale from a whisky sour.

Nor is it the case that because Hesketh was inclined to be indulgently disposed towards his subjects he was incapable of seeing their faults, or of avoiding taking a prejudiced view of related characters who were, for him, in Charles Lamb's expression,

imperfect sympathies. Thus, in his book on Conan
Doyle he manages – a rare feat – to be fair to Dr
Watson, and in his *Labby* to see the point of Bradlaugh.
This present volume is a case in point. It is obvious
that he greatly preferred Gilbert to Sullivan, who
had certain traits which to Hesketh were particularly
abhorrent. For instance, he took himself and his work
with deadly seriousness, assiduously sought the
company of royal and aristocratic personages, and
tended to despise the enchanting melodies he
produced to match Gilbert's sparkling verses which
brought both of them fame and wealth, actually preferring his own heavy-handed productions like *The
Lost Chord*. Gilbert, on the other hand, had all the
characteristics Hesketh most appreciated. That is to
say, he never could resist making a joke however
disastrous the consequences; he was impulsive,
sometimes choleric, disrespectful, and recklessly
extravagent and generous with his money. Even so,
Hesketh manages, with a decided effort, I admit, to
hold the balance evenly between them, recognizing
Gilbert's faults of selfishness and inconsiderateness,
and acknowledging Sullivan's virtues of consideration
for others, especially his family, and conscientiousness
about his work.

I am quite sure it would have greatly pleased
Hesketh to know that his *Gilbert and Sullivan* was to
be in the first batch of his books to be republished.
His delight in the operas never flagged, and a revival
of *The Mikardo*, *Patience* or *The Gondoliers* – his

favourites – always found him in the audience. For his surviving friends and multitude of admirers, it is most welcome news that his books are again to be in print and available, and for me personally a special pleasure and privilege to have been given the opportunity to add these words by way of Introduction to one of them.

Malcolm Muggeridge
March 1975

AUTHOR'S FOREWORD

THERE are plenty of books dealing with the works of Gilbert and Sullivan; my book deals with the lives and personalities of Gilbert and Sullivan.

Apart from the list of authorities cited at the end, I wish to acknowledge with sincere thanks the help I have received from Miss Jessie Bond, Mr. Jack Robertson and Mr. Bernard Shaw.

CHAPTER I

GILBERT

1

THE office-boy paused in the act of stamping a letter and glanced towards the door, which was flung open violently by a choleric-looking gentleman, who advanced to the centre of the room and said in a threatening tone:

"I wish to see the editor of the *Saturday Review*."

"On what business, sir?"

"To thrash him."

The editor, as usual in such circumstances, was "out," and the angry gentleman, after making an appointment for the following morning with a similar object in view, stormed out of the office. We do not know whether that appointment was kept (the editor was a busy man) but we do know that the caller's name was William Gilbert, a retired naval surgeon who wrote a quantity of plays, tracts, poems, biographies and three-volume novels, one of which had been severely dealt with by the *Saturday Review*, that his favourite theme was insanity and that his son wrote *The Mikado*.

Publishers, no less than editors, viewed his visits with uneasiness. He had been known to call and personally destroy every copy of a work containing a few typographical errors, and it was fairly generally felt among members of the trade that his anxiety on this occasion had been excessive. Of his wife nothing is known; but if the morbid activity that distinguished him was alien to her nature, she probably succumbed to the fate so strongly deprecated by Falstaff and was "scoured to nothing by perpetual motion."

Their son, William, who objected to his second name "Schwenck" so much that we had better forget it, was born at No. 17 Southampton Street, Strand, on the 18th of November, 1836. He had three sisters and no brothers. His first experience of comic opera came to him at the age of two, when he was with his parents at Naples. Two courteous Italians stopped his nurse in the road and informed her that the English gentleman had sent them to fetch the baby. Captivated by their pleasant speech and charming manners, the nurse did not hesitate for a moment, but made them a present of William, who was then carried through some fine mountain scenery, which impressed him so much that he remembered it when visiting the country in after-years, and a request for the equivalent of twenty-five pounds sterling was despatched to his parents. He was redeemed by return and about forty years later made use of the incident in a less realistic form.

After a little preliminary study at Boulogne he was sent, at the age of thirteen, to the Great Ealing school, where Thackeray, Marryat, Newman and Huxley had learnt their grammar. Here he displayed certain features of a character that never appreciably matured. He was cross-grained, quick to take offence, and his inclination to punch the head of anyone who did not agree with him resulted in frequent combats. He wrote a number of plays, which were performed by fellow-pupils, and we may be sure that the friction at rehearsals did not make him less unpopular.

Believing that, given the chance, he could teach real actors a thing or two, he decided to waste no more time over the classics, but to go on the stage at once. Without communicating this bright idea to anyone in authority, he left school one afternoon and made his way to the theatre where the leading actor of the day, Charles Kean, was performing. Once in the theatre, he became the prey of misgivings, and when at last Kean appeared he was not in a condition to bear up against the actor's voice, which, though it sounded splendid in the gallery, was more like the roar of exploding gunpowder at close quarters.

"So you would like to be an act-orrr?" bellowed Kean.

"Ye—e—es."

"What's yourrr name?"

Gilbert tried hard to think of any name except
his own, but the eagle eye of the actor was upon
him and he faltered out an apologetic "G-Gilbert."

"Not the son of me old frrriend, Gilbert?"

The fat was in the fire.

"Ye—es."

Gilbert was back among the classics the following
morning.

Lazy by nature, he continued to neglect his
lessons until it occurred to him that he was being
left behind by a number of fellows whose brains he
despised; whereupon he pulled himself together,
began to win prizes, and by the age of sixteen had
become head boy of the school.

From Ealing he went to King's College, meaning
to finish up at Oxford; but the war in the Crimea
aroused his military ardour, and after taking his
degree he began to work hard for a direct commis-
sion in the Royal Artillery. It was fortunate for the
cause of Comic Opera that, to use his own words,
"the Crimean war wouldn't wait whilst the authorities were deciding how good a gunner I would
make," and at the sudden termination of hostilities
he obtained by examination an assistant clerkship
in the Education Department of the Privy Council
Office, where, on a salary of £120 a year, he spent
four thoroughly unhappy years. He hated the

routine, the red tape and the necessity of being polite to his seniors. "I was one of the worst bargains any Government ever made," he declared. He tried to make life bearable by playing practical jokes on the inhabitants of the Pimlico boarding-house where he lived and by throwing out mysterious hints to his fellow-clerks that he exercised considerable influence in the world of the theatre. One of the latter, much impressed, approached him with a request:

"Could you write me an order for the play, Mr. Gilbert?"

"Of course I could. What shall I write it for—stalls or a box?"

"A box, if you please."

Gilbert promptly wrote the order.

Next day the clerk approached him with a different expression on his face and a different sort of request. He had taken his wife and family to the theatre, had presented Gilbert's order, had been mortified by the laughter with which it was received, and wanted to know what Gilbert meant by it?

"I did precisely what you asked me to do," Gilbert replied. "You asked me whether I could write you an order for the play. I replied that I could, and in fact I did; but I never said it would be of the least use to you."

Practical joking did not entirely absorb his

energies, which were partly expended on peaceful warfare. He joined the Militia and became an officer in the 3rd Battalion of the Gordon High-landers. He served in the Militia for nearly twenty years, making an efficient and picturesque officer on parade, and only drawing the line at personal discomfort. During one field-day in Scotland, when the weather was particularly moist and unpleasant, he was ordered to take his men to a certain place. The "enemy" were duly apprised of his supposed direction, and a considerable force hunted him through bog, heather and burn. At the end of a very tiring day, having failed to locate him, the hostile force returned to headquarters, wet through and limp from exhaustion, only to find Gilbert and his men sitting comfortably round their various firesides, where they had spent the better part of the day. Gilbert explained that there was no plea-sure in tramping about through a Scotch mist, so he had brought his men straight home.

Though his influence in theatrical quarters was not so wide as he liked to pretend, the stage and the concert-hall were his chief interests in life, and in 1857 his first song was not only sung but printed. From childhood he had known a popular singer named Mlle Parepa, who now asked him to do a translation of the laughing-song from *Manon Lescaut*. This she sang night after night to great applause at Mellon's Promenade Concerts, and Gilbert went to hear her, night after night, in order to stand close to some promenader who was following the song in the programme and to enjoy the thrill of imagining what that interested mortal would say if only he could know that the genius who had written the very words he was reading was actually at his elbow. Gilbert's subsequent experience taught him that the mortal in question would probably have received the information with fortitude.

2

At last his four years of servitude came to an end. He inherited four hundred pounds from an aunt, and on the happiest day of his life sent in his resignation. Having thus emancipated himself from what he described as "the detestable thraldom of this baleful office," he paid a hundred pounds for the privilege of being a student at the Inner Temple, a hundred pounds to be a pupil in the chambers of Mr. Watkin Wilkins (afterwards a judge), another hundred pounds for his fee of admission to the Bar, and the final hundred pounds to set himself up in chambers in Clement's Inn. Though Gilbert never lost his interest in the law, it cannot be said that the law took much interest in him. Business was never brisk. He practised for four years, averaged about five clients a year, and earned seventy-five pounds in all. He was a clumsy and nervous speaker and seldom earned the gratitude of his clients, though on one occasion, much to his embarrassment, he was hugged and kissed in open court by a Frenchman whose cause he had won.

His first appearance as a barrister was at Liverpool, and for a novice the experience was a little trying. Rather over-estimating his powers as a prosecuting counsel and forgetful of the fact that a court, unlike a theatre, was an arena for unrehearsed effects, he asked Mr. and Mrs. Bancroft and their touring company to witness the proceedings. The first delinquent was an Irish woman, charged with stealing a coat, and the moment Gilbert was on his legs she decided that he was not there for her good.

"Ah, ye devil, sit down!" she shouted. "Don't listen to him, yer honner! He's known in all the slums of Liverpool! Sit down, ye spalpeen! He's as drunk as a lord, yer honner, begging yer lordship's pardon!"

Every attempt he made to speak was drowned by her eloquence, and at last he threw himself on the protection of the Recorder, who was too helpless with laughter to interfere. Eventually he managed to deliver his maiden speech, which, possibly because the court felt the contest to be unfair, was rewarded with three months for the more eloquent of the protagonists.

He was not very fortunate in his legal collisions with members of the fair sex. His first brief was on behalf of a lady who had been accused of picking a pocket in an omnibus. This lady was of a religious turn of mind; in fact she was on her way to attend a tea-and-prayer meeting when a fellow-traveller made the accusation, and sure enough the latter's purse was found in the good woman's pocket. Gilbert was impressed by his client's religious habits and by her statement that she always carried a hymn-book in that pocket. He therefore assumed that the purse had been "planted" on her person, and cross-examined the policeman who made the arrest with the easy assurance of one who knew all the relevant facts.

"You say you found the purse in her pocket, my man?"

"Yes, sir."

"Did you find anything else?"

"Yes, sir."

"What?"

"Two other purses, a watch with the bow broken, three handkerchiefs, two silver pencil-cases, and a hymn-book."

The recital of this catalogue was punctuated with roars of laughter in court, and the exhibits proved that Gilbert's client was not solely interested in spiritual matters.

"You may stand down," he said.

His speech was necessarily confined to an expression of his deep personal conviction of the prisoner's innocence, on which he was willing to stake his professional reputation; and after declaring his confidence in a verdict that would restore the maligned lady to an admiring circle of private friends, several of whom were waiting in the court below to testify to her excellent character, he sat down.

"Call witnesses to Mrs. Briggs's character," he then commanded, knowing perfectly well that the only witnesses in the building had already given incriminating evidence.

The crier shouted the words, which were repeated several times in the corridors without. But no one seemed anxious to testify.

"Dear, dear," said Gilbert, after a long pause, "this is really most unfortunate. They must have mistaken the day."

"Shouldn't wonder," remarked the prosecuting counsel.

The sentence of eighteen months' hard labour was scarcely out of the judge's mouth before Mrs. Briggs stooped down, pulled off a heavy boot, and flung it at her counsel's head, following it up with a stream of invective surprising in a lady devoted to prayer and sacred song. The boot missed Gilbert, but caught a reporter on a sensitive spot, and to this fact Gilbert attributed the unfavourable light in which his efforts for the defence were viewed by several of the papers next morning.

An embrace from a gentleman and a boot from a lady did not encourage Gilbert to believe that he had found his true vocation, and during these briefless years he began to write and to draw. With a packet of quill pens, a few wood blocks, and a quire or two of blue foolscap paper at his side, he spent the hours waiting for clients in writing and illustrating articles for the weekly papers. Nearly all were returned with the usual editorial regret. Deciding that his work was better than the stuff that was published by editors without regret, he sent it direct to certain magazine proprietors, who agreed with him and insisted that his articles should be accepted. This did not make him popular with editors or their staffs, but he was quite willing to put up with that so long as his work continued to appear.

In 1861 a paper called *Fun* was started with H. J. Byron as editor. It became a serious rival to *Punch*, and its humour was of the same order. Byron was famous as the writer of farces, one of which, *Our Boys*, had a success that was only surpassed at a later date by *Charley's Aunt*. Byron's idea of fun was a pun, and the more execrable the pun the more uproarious the fun. "I don't like *cock*roaches," he once said, "because they "*en*-croaches," and the laughter lasted for several

minutes. A character in one of his plays, speaking
of nectar, declared:

"It's called divine—this is *de vine* for me," and the
audience was reduced to hysteria.

Gilbert saw at once that *Fun* was the paper for
him, and forestalled the editor's regrets by sending
an illustrated article to the proprietor. In spite of
the fact that he was told to accept it, Byron liked
it well enough to engage Gilbert as a permanent
contributor. At first his fellow-contributors looked
upon him with disfavour; he had become one of
their number by what they regarded as underhand
means; he was not, like themselves, a born journa-
list; he was an interloper, an outsider; and he was
treated with scant courtesy at the weekly *Fun*
dinners. Gilbert set himself to remedy this state of
affairs. Moving to chambers in South Square,
Gray's Inn, he founded a small coterie of young
dramatists, critics and journalists, which was called
"The Serious Family." Tom Hood (who succeeded
Byron as editor of *Fun*) was elected father of the
family, Gilbert became known as the *enfant terrible*,
and H. J. Byron, Clement Scott, Tom Robertson,
Artemus Ward and a score of others made up the
family circle.

They met weekly in Gilbert's chambers and the
annual subscription was two guineas, from the payment of which Gilbert alone was exempted, on the
understanding that he should supply a rump steak

pie, a joint of cold boiled beef, a Stilton cheese, whisky and soda and bottled ale, every Saturday night for the rest of his life; an expensive way of becoming popular, though it probably paid him to know the sort of people it paid to know. Robertson was soon to become the leading dramatist of the age, Scott its leading critic, and Gilbert had a quick eye for rising talent.

3

Gilbert wrote all sorts of articles for *Fun*: dramatic criticisms, art criticisms, stories, poetry, and even, on one occasion, a savage political satire on Napoleon III, in which one detects the view that the Emperor's real crime was that he had never learnt how to behave like a standard English gentleman. Gilbert also did many illustrations for *Fun*, the best of them being those with which the famous *Bab Ballads* went forth into the world. As a child he had been called "Bab" by his family, and in adopting the nickname as a pseudonym he unconsciously disclosed a curious quality in the Ballads. In certain respects they are the offspring of a juvenile mentality. We are not here concerned with their many verbal and metrical felicities, which have been pointed out by innumerable critics. What does concern us is the light they shed upon the personality of their creator.

The first thing that must strike the careful reader is that they are full of a playful, school-boyish cruelty, the sort of cruelty that derives satisfaction in hearing about the acute discomfort of someone else or laughs with pleasure at the sight of it. But what is merely primitive in a boy is morbid in a man, and its presence in the grown-up Gilbert is partly due to his own nature and partly to the age in which he lived. His personality, we have already seen, was domineering and self-assertive; he was a born fighter and conqueror; if he could not get what he wanted by ordinary means, he put his back into the business and achieved it by extraordinary effort; he despised competitors and always wanted to go one better than their best. Though personally sensitive, he cared little about the feelings of others. He had a high opinion of his own ability and a low opinion of the ability of nearly everyone else, though he was attracted to Dickens, sometimes did him the unique honour of quoting the sayings of his characters, and dramatised *Great Expectations*. In brief, Gilbert was a strong, full-blooded, impatient and irreverent Englishman, which accounts for some of the vindictiveness and callousness in the *Bab Ballads*.

But he was also an essentially proper person who was writing in the eighteen-sixties, a period of prudery, spiritual fog and mental perversity un-exampled in English history, when humour that had any connection with real life was regarded with grave suspicion, when the subject of sex was banned as obscene, and when the rest of Europe was supposed to be living in sin.

While conforming to his own sense of propriety and the oppressive influences of the age, Gilbert partially appeased his lust for position and possession by deflecting it into an orgy of fanciful sadism, which appeared to be of so topsy-turvy a nature, so unlike the respectable façade of the stolid mid-Victorian world, that his readers found relief in laughter over this inverted picture of their own conscious or subconscious desires.

It is worth recalling that Mark Lemon, the editor of *Punch*, refused to accept *The Yarn of the Nancy Bell* on the ground that it was too cannibalistic for the taste of his readers, and his refusal has been treated by later critics as one of the jokes of the century. But it is clear that he sensed something in Gilbert's poetry that made him feel a little uncomfortable (strong meat, perhaps, that had "turned" in the sultry weather of that Victorian noontide), and though Gilbert's more vegetarian style was perfectly adapted to the humour of *Punch*, the distinguishing feature of which might be described as lack of punch, we may do Mark Lemon belated justice by saying that his sense of smell was more acute than that of his contemporaries.

In Gilbert there was a ceaseless warfare between

daring and discretion; his natural bluntness was sharply counteracted by his sense of business; his violent tempers were instantly followed by an assuaging charm. After writing certain dramatic criticisms which to-day would have subjected him to legal proceedings (e.g. "That dismal actor Mr. Jordan was playing . . . and it is impossible to say how much his depressing presence may have told upon the animal spirits of the audience"), he suddenly realised that this kind of thing might prove hurtful to his own career and promptly stopped writing on the theatre, giving the reason that he did not like being hated, which was the doom of any critic who told the truth.

Since he had written fifteen plays by the age of twenty-four, in one of which there were eighteen scenes, four cataracts and a house on fire, we may guess that his mind was centred on the stage and that in order to get a drama produced he had decided to play up to the actors instead of writing them down. He maintained a close alliance with Tom Robertson, the leading dramatist of the 'sixties, who allowed Gilbert to witness his methods of production. This was immensely helpful, because Robertson was the first of the modern producers in England. Before his time stage-management, as we understand it to-day, was non-existent. In a pre-Robertson play, for example, when it became necessary for several characters to indulge in a little intimate conversation, the actors brought forward their chairs from the side or back of the stage, sat down, completed their talk, got up, replaced the chairs, and the drama proceeded with no furniture to cramp the performer's style. Robertson altered all that. He made each scene an integral part of the play, giving it life and animation by the introduction of movement and by-play. Gilbert admired his methods of production and his skill as a playwright, but naturally determined to go one better in both spheres of energy.

Gilbert's plays are not only dead, but buried, and they are never likely to be resurrected except perhaps as fossils of an extinct species. For our purpose it is enough to say that most of them are drenched in false sentiment, which expresses the author's overcharged emotions in the acceptable medium of the age, and are placed in a fanciful setting, which expresses his real hatred of the mid-Victorian world and equally real dread lest his personal feelings might burst through the mock-mist of prudery that surrounded him. He once said that no play-story was decent that could not be told at a mixed dinner-party. This may account for the fact that in the present age, when very few stories told at a mixed dinner-party could be repeated on the stage, mid-Victorian dramas are regarded as burlesques.

The first of his plays to be produced was written

to order on the advice of Tom Robertson, who was thus his theatrical godfather as well as his chief influence as producer and playwright. Gilbert finished it in a few days, and under the title of *Dulcamara* it appeared at the St. James's Theatre on December the 29th, 1866. Only thirty years of age, and therefore sanguine of success, Gilbert invited a few friends to supper after the performance. Fortunately, the play was well received and the party was an appropriate close to a happy evening; but having experienced a number of less pleasant "first nights," an older and sadder Gilbert declared that he "would as soon invite friends to supper after a forthcoming amputation at the hip-joint." The play was written and put on in a hurry and the subject of author's royalties was not raised until after it had been successfully produced. Then the manager asked Gilbert how much he wanted for the piece. Gilbert made a careful mental reckoning: three days' work at three guineas a day; incidentals, say ten guineas more; and another ten to go on with.

"Thirty guineas," he suggested.

"Oh, dear, no!" said the manager; "we never pay in guineas. You must make it pounds."

"Very well," agreed Gilbert.

The manager wrote out a cheque, handed it to Gilbert, and said: "Now take a bit of advice from an old stager who knows what he is talking about:

never sell so good a piece as this for thirty pounds again."

Gilbert never did.

Once launched on the theatrical stream, he sailed right ahead. During the next dozen years comedies, dramas, farces, burlesques, plays in blank verse, plays in stilted prose, plays in rhymed couplets, flowed from his pen, and it is difficult to say whether the Elizabethan dramatists would have been more amazed by their quantity or their quality. Sometimes he even appeared as an actor, and though reports conflict as to his skill in that department, some calling him the worst actor that ever appeared on a stage, others describing him as a most capable player, it is probable that John Hollingshead got fairly near the mark when he said that Gilbert as Harlequin gave a good idea of what Oliver Cromwell would have made of the character.

His appearance as Harlequin was in a matinee performance for the benefit of the Royal General Theatrical Fund, and we get an early glimpse of Gilbert rehearsing his play *The Vagabond* on the morning of the same day. One of the actors, Mr. (afterwards Sir) Johnston Forbes-Robertson, not quite sure of his lines, was falling back on his own vocabulary, when Gilbert suddenly said: "You don't know your words!" The actor rejoined that Gilbert had better get someone else for the part.

The matter went no further at the moment, and Forbes-Robertson hoped that the incident was closed. But he reckoned without his author. A little later, in a love-scene with Marion Terry, he asked if he might rise from the log on which he was seated. "Oh, you may stand on your head if you like!" snapped Gilbert. "No, I leave that to you," replied the other, feeling sure that Gilbert's forthcoming appearance in pantomime would clarify the point. It did. Gilbert was furious with himself for having given Forbes-Robertson such an excellent opening, and did not speak to him for thirty years. At the close of that period, during which the author had frequently seen and glared at the actor in the Garrick Club, a letter proposing a reconciliation came from Gilbert, and the two were quickly on excellent terms.

We shall find that Gilbert, at the end of his life, did his best to patch up ancient quarrels and to disown the many acid sayings attributed to him. He succeeded so well that many of his most famous gibes are now commonly regarded as apochryphal. But the mellowing picture of an ageing man, anxious above all things to conciliate his contemporaries and to leave the world in an odour of charity and good-will, must not be accepted as an accurate representation of the younger man whose restless desire to achieve pre-eminence set him at odds with all who would not bow to his will and whose jealousy of the success of others expressed itself in a wit that cut like a whip. There is quite enough authentic evidence for the truth of his recorded sarcasms to justify their inclusion in the most prudent biography.

4

People who are not sure of their own beliefs or their own integrity frequently preach to others in order to reassure themselves. The majority of moralists have a strong sense of personal guilt and many prophets have been made by their own lack of conviction. Gilbert would have been a stern moralist if only he had been given the chance. But having once laughed with him, the public refused to take him seriously, and he was furious over the failure of his sentimental plays, which did express something very strongly felt by himself; and though he was never quite certain what that something was, it worried him to the end of his life. He was of course profoundly disturbed by the humbug and hypocrisy of his age, but tempera- mentally he belonged to it, and the strife between his intelligence and his emotions produced an internal confusion, a see-saw of feelings and an uncertainty of aim, which in turn produced his outrageous burlesques, his sentimental comedies, and, after a period of enforced discipline, his excellent libretti.

We need not linger over his early works beyond noting that, in a wildly farcical mood, he created a doleful queen who said;

> I wander, dressing-gowny and night-cappy,
> I seldom get a nap—I'm so un-nappy!

and that, in a very serious mood, he created a woman who, because she had once been to bed with a man, spent the rest of her life in self-sacrifice to redeem her respectability.

Gilbert's personality appears more definitely in his life than in his art, and the first thing to observe is that he was subject to fits of fury that made him enemies on every side. His anger was caused, not only by the disunion of mind and heart that made him abnormally sensitive to any form of criticism or disagreement, but also by the fact that he was not the dominant person at rehearsals of his plays. Until the great days of Savoy Opera he had to deal with "stars" who were much more important than himself and who had their own views as to how their parts should be played. Now Gilbert could not bear a second Cæsar in the theatre, and be-haved like a spoilt child when his advice was ignored or his opinions were gainsaid.

He had a particular affection for one of his

sentimental plays, *Broken Hearts*, and believed that
he had put more of his real self into it than into
any of his operas. The scene is set on an island
where four broken-hearted maidens, whose lovers
have died and who are pledged never to love again
(except some inanimate object), have taken refuge.
A handsome young man lands on the island; two
of the maidens fall in love with him; and after each
has tried to outdo the other in unselfishness, the
younger obligingly dies and leaves the handsome
young man to her sister. The constant repetition
of exalted sentiments has a most dispiriting effect
on fallible human beings, and it is not surprising
to learn that during the rehearsals of this play
John Hare, the actor, and William Gilbert, the
author, developed the habit of flying into a temper
on the slightest provocation. Once they quarrelled
so violently that each of them left the Court
Theatre for the Underground Railway, stamped
angrily up and down the same platform while
waiting for a train, suddenly decided to make it
up, shook hands, returned to the theatre with the
intention of continuing the rehearsal, and found
that the company had gone home.

Gilbert must have been vaguely conscious that
this play left something to be desired, because he
became quite touchy on the subject, and when
F. Burnand told Clement Scott that he was just
off to see Gilbert's *Broken Parts*, and Scott thought

the joke good enough to quote in an article, Gilbert wrote an angry letter to the effect that the article was offensive and in the worst possible taste, that Burnand's attempt at wit was coarse and silly, that he (Gilbert) was not a thin-skinned man, but that he felt bound to take exception to such treatment of him and his serious work. Thereafter Gilbert was not on speaking terms with Scott, though when the famous dramatic critic was dying Gilbert's sentiment got the better of him; he called at the house every day, and after Scott's death helped his widow in countless ways, besides weeping copiously at the funeral. He did not altogether break with Burnand, though he never quite forgave him, and there was a famous (and always misquoted) clash between the two at the house of Sir Squire Bancroft, when another guest asked: .

"Mr. Burnand, do you ever receive for *Punch* good jokes and things from outsiders?"

"Oh, often!" said Burnand.

"They never appear," grunted Gilbert from the opposite side of the table.

Burnand succeeded Mark Lemon as editor of *Punch*. He was famous for practical jokes, one of which was so frequently retailed by Gilbert that it must be instanced here as the type of humour he most enjoyed.

Burnand was giving a dinner-party, and the first to arrive was J. L. Toole, the actor. While they were chatting together voices were heard on the stairs outside.

"Get under the table, Toole," whispered Burnand urgently: "quick, man, quick!"

The comedian, after a momentary pause of surprise, scented a joke and did as requested.

Several people entered the room, then a few more, and at last, when Burnand announced that the party was complete, one of the guests remarked:

"But I thought you were expecting Toole to-night?"

"Oh, yes; he is here," replied Burnand.

"Here? Where?"

"Under the table."

"Under the table? Whatever for?"

"Blessed if I know!" said Burnand with a shrug; "you'd better ask him."

Whereat the disconcerted face of Toole appeared from beneath the table-cloth, the rest of him followed, the company were delighted, and a full explanation of his undignified conduct made their laughter all the heartier.

Another play of Gilbert's that resulted in more friction than fun, though it made him a fortune, was *Pygmalion and Galatea*, in which Madge Robertson (sister of Tom Robertson and afterwards Dame Madge Kendal) acted in 1871. Madge Robertson played leading parts in several of his plays, and being a lady with a will of her own, they were soon at loggerheads. Gilbert's revenge was peculiar: he would sometimes appear with a party in the stage box and pay the closest attention to the acting of the other members of the cast; but the moment Miss Robertson came on the scene he would turn his back to the stage and talk audibly with his friends, punctuating the conversation with loud laughs.

Pygmalion and Galatea was often revived, and another actress, Janette Steer, who had dared to depart from the traditional "business," became the object of the author's wrath. He wrote her a letter explaining in detail where she had gone wrong and closing with the threat: "If you do not comply with my wishes in these respects I give you notice that on Monday I shall apply for an injunction to prevent your playing the piece." Janette did as she was told, but determined to teach him a lesson and to make things difficult for the actress who had complained of her behaviour. She therefore uttered several exclamations during a long speech delivered by her hated rival, causing the speaker to lose her temper and become confused. Whereupon Gilbert informed Janette that he had told the other actress exactly how she was to deal with the exclamations should they occur again: she was to stop short at the first interruption, remain silent till it ceased, then begin again, and should the nuisance be repeated to stop altogether until it was discontinued.

We do not know whether the audience demanded their money back.

Trouble seemed to accompany *Pygmalion and Galatea* for when Mary Anderson revived it in the 'eighties (Gilbert by then a great power in the land), she could not see eye-to-eye with the author. Already she had appeared as Galatea with success in America, but Gilbert told her quite frankly that she would not be tolerated by the London public. She wished to play the part in the classic style, as though it retained some of its statue-quality, but Gilbert said it was a nineteenth century comedy dressed in Greek costume, which was the only classical thing about it, and she must be alive and up-to-date. Result: tears and tempers. The strained atmosphere was not improved by Henry Kemble, a fearless and downright actor, who had a difference of opinion with the producer and said: "Doubtless you think yourself a very clever person, Mr. Gilbert, but I, for one, fail to see it." The company was aghast, the rehearsal was stopped, and the manager led Mr. Gilbert out to the nearest restaurant, where he revived over a lunch.

Later there was discordance over the dresses. Alma-Tadema designed some draperies for Mary Anderson in the style of the Tanagra figures. Gilbert said that she looked like a stiff mediæval saint. Nothing she could say or do seemed to satisfy him, and she became so depressed that as she
B*

drove to and from the theatre she envied the old
women who were sweeping the streets.   At the
final dress-rehearsal she tried pose after pose in the
Alma-Tadema draperies, but Gilbert remained
hostile.   She arrived in her dressing-room before
the first performance in a state of utter dejection
and spent an hour or two before the long mirror,
with swollen eyes and tear-stained face, trying on
some white drapery that had been bought and
fashioned by her mother at the last moment.
Then she had her reward.   The audience received
her appearance with round after round of applause.
Wilkie Collins was so much moved that his hands
grew as cold as ice and his heart thumped as if it
would fly out of him, and even Gilbert had to
admit that she had made a great success.   But he
was haunted by the belief that the box office
receipts were due to her conception of the part, not
his; and though he was enough of a business man
to want her to produce his next play, *Brantinghame
Hall*, he displayed his pique when she declined it
by asking whether she found anything gross in it,
adding: "I hear you hate gross things so much
that you can hardly be induced to take your share
of the gross receipts."

5

The tale of quarrels and reconciliations, of the quick substitutions of charm for irritability, of lifelong hostilities and last-minute repentances, goes on all through Gilbert's life. We hear of him having a row with an actor who was about to make an entrance on a trap-door, knocking him down, taking his place without a moment's hesitation, popping up on the trap-door, to the consternation of the other actors, and playing the part without turning a hair. We also hear of his consideration for actresses, whose cab-fares home he would pay after late rehearsals when the last buses had gone. But chiefly, in those early days, we are made aware of something strangely mutable in his character, of a want of consistency and an utter incapacity for self-control, remarkable in a man of his will-power and determination. The truth has already been hinted: his brain was not in harmony with his sentiments; he was a child of his age who saw through his age; and so he fought, not for any reason, but for the sake of the fight. This gave him an indirectness of aim throughout his life; he hit out in all directions, not caring who or what he hit; he had no positive beliefs and no positive disbeliefs; he neither believed nor disbelieved in W. S. Gilbert, though he thought him a good deal better than his contemporaries.

The lack of any central motive in him is perfectly illustrated in his quarrel with Henrietta Hodson, who afterwards became Mrs. Henry Labouchere. The trouble began in 1874, when Miss Hodson produced a play in which Gilbert had collaborated at the Royalty Theatre. Having lost his temper at rehearsals, Gilbert complained to someone that Miss Hodson had a habit of using bad language. This was repeated to Miss Hodson, who promptly called upon Gilbert to apologise. After some pressure he did so. Rather injudiciously Miss Hodson distributed copies of his apology among those whom it might concern. Gilbert, infuriated, used his influence to prevent her appearing in a revival of *Pgymalion and Galatea* at the Haymarket Theatre three years later, though she was then a permanent member of the company. Naturally she complained of persecution. The situation was slightly complicated by the fact that a printseller, Mr. Graves, who financed the theatre, insisted on a certain lady friend of his playing the leading part; but it is perfectly clear that Gilbert, whose anger would normally have been aroused by such a proceeding, took advantage of this in order to oust Miss Hodson.

The quarrel got into the papers, and for some weeks *The Theatre* printed Miss Hodson's avowals and Gilbert's rejoinders. Gilbert said that he had always treated Miss Hodson with "studied courtesy," a treatment which Miss Hodson described as "studied insult." Her declared object was to force Gilbert to take legal proceedings against her, and to this end she publicly accused him of exercising a sort of terrorism over the dramatic profession, of threatening managers who had produced his pieces with actions if they declined to run them for a certain number of consecutive weeks at a heavy nightly loss, of "cutting" critics who had dared to express their honest opinions of his plays, of bullying actors and frightening them into submission with the threat that they would never again appear in his pieces. Further, she revealed that she had heard from his own lips that he had quarrelled with everyone with whom he had been professionally connected, that he had forced actresses who had resented his behaviour to eat mud pie, and that he considered himself superior to Shakespeare in dramatic gifts.

In reply Gilbert said that he was not responsible for the casting at the Haymarket Theatre, and he printed a letter from Buckstone, the manager, which proved that he had not acted in opposition to Miss Hodson's interests; to which the latter retorted: "You are fully capable of either having dictated it to him or of having forged it to suit your own purposes." A man more sure of himself would have acted promptly at this point, but Gilbert shifted evasively from one position to another, now putting the responsibility on to someone else, now introducing matters that were not in dispute, now producing testimonials to his rectitude. His constant references to correspondence which seemed to demonstrate his innocence drew from her the statement that he kept a copy-book in which appeared copies of letters he had *not* posted to people.

Throughout the controversy she referred to him as Mr. William *Schwenck* Gilbert, which did not forward a reconciliation, but not even the irritating repetition of his curious Christian name forced his hand. Letters flew to and from the solicitors of the injured parties, but Gilbert kept out of court, and the end of it was that he received a solemn editorial admonition in *The Theatre*: "Mr. Gilbert has yet to learn that he is a servant of the public and amenable to public opinion." Mr. Graves was also sharply reprimanded for pressing the histrionic claims of a lady "in whose fortunes he is pleased to take a warm interest"; and then the incident blew over.

After associating with actors and managers for a number of years, Gilbert wrote and published a scathing sketch of their leading characteristics In this sketch an author is tried for the crime of writing an unsuccessful play and evidence is given by the manager of the theatre wherein it was produced and by various members of the cast. The manager has to explain why he put the play on: "I was at my wits' end. I have been there before. I soon get there. I have had no special training for the position of manager. I am not aware that any special training is requisite. It is a very easy profession to master. If you make a success, you pocket the profits; if you fail, you close your theatre abruptly, and a benefit performance is organised on your behalf. Then you begin again." The leading lady is made to say that "Two minor parts were fused with mine to make it worthy of my reputation. I did not charge extra for rolling the three parts into one. I did it entirely in the author's interest. I do not remember his objecting to the mutilation of his play. It is not a circumstance that would be likely to dwell in my mind. I have never been hissed in my life. The parts I have played have frequently been hissed. No one has ever hissed me." The low comedian assures the court that he did his best with a very inferior part: "In my zeal on behalf of the prisoner I introduced much practical 'business.' I introduced it solely in the prisoner's interest. No doubt the prisoner remonstrated, but I knew what an audience likes better than he does." The lady who played the part of a sad-hearted governess, secretly in love with the Home Secretary, explains why the governess broke into a song and dance in the intervals between her pathetic scenes: "She might be supposed to do so in order to cheer her spirits."

There are limits, she admits, but truth to nature demands an occasional song and dance from a depressed person. And then she deals with another of the author's complaints: "I wore short petticoats because the audience expected it of me. I see no reason why a governess in a country vicarage should not wear short petticoats if she has good legs."

From these extracts we can see that Gilbert, though hot-tempered, had some cause for his outbursts in the theatre of the 'seventies, and his reputation for irascibility may be partly due to the accommodating methods of other authors who did not mind seeing their plays mangled. Of course Gilbert over-estimated the value of his serious plays, but he was right to insist that they should be performed as he wrote them; and even when he was aware that he had not done his best (e.g. his version of the Faust story, of which he said: "I called it *Gretchen*, the public called it rot") no actor could misquote him without provoking an explosion.

He did not become a leading dramatist without a great deal of hard work and a lot of disappointment. Many of his early plays were returned so promptly that it crossed his mind they had not been read by the managers concerned. To make certain of this he tried an experiment on Horace Wigan, the manager of the Olympic, to whom he sent the script of his play *The Princess*, a blank-verse burlesque of Tennyson's poem, with the middle pages carefully gummed together. A few days later Wigan handed it back to him with the remark that it was unsuitable.

"Did you read it?" queried Gilbert.

"Of course," Wigan replied in a hurt tone of voice.

"By gum, you didn't!" said Gilbert, displaying the pages and the adhesive substance which proved the fact.

6

In 1867 Gilbert married the daughter of an Indian officer, Miss Lucy Blois Turner, and after the successful production of *The Princess* had brought him to the front they took a house at No. 24 The Boltons, South Kensington, which, though they had no children of their own, soon became famous for its children's parties, whereat Gilbert the stage-martinet would not have been recognised by his professional associates. By the middle of the 'seventies he was a famous and successful dramatist, could afford to ride in the Row, had bought a pleasant little yacht, and was a member of the Junior Carlton Club. Not being interested in the subject, he took his politics from his club and called himself a Conservative. He was fond of riding, and once rebuked a fellow-equestrian in Hyde Park who was nervous of trotting or galloping: "Take care, or you'll be had up by the

police for furious loitering!" His happiest hours
were spent on the yacht with his wife and a friend
or two, braving all weathers and only complaining
when his cook suffered from the delusion that "the
more you water gravy, the more gravy you get."
But all through these years he was an extremely
busy man, writing so many plays that in later life
he claimed the authorship of over seventy, many no
doubt having been mislaid or forgotten by that
time, among them a number of duologues, operettas and so forth written for the German Reeds,
who gave a popular entertainment at the Gallery
of Illustration in Lower Regent Street, and under
whose management the famous Corney Grain first
burst upon the town as a drawing-room entertainer.

One day in the autumn of 1870 Fred Clay, who
had composed the music to several of Gilbert's
operettas, introduced him to another composer at
the Gallery of Illustration. This was Arthur
Sullivan, whose music for *The Tempest* had made a
sensation. Gilbert had just completed a blank-
verse play called *The Palace of Truth* for the Haymarket Theatre, in which one of the characters was
a musical pedant. Knowing nothing about music,
Gilbert had read the article on Harmony in the
Encyclopædia Britannica, had taken a long sentence
from it, and without the least notion of its meaning
had turned it into blank-verse. Curious to know

whether a passage that sounded like nonsense to him would pass muster with a distinguished musician, he switched it back into prose and fired it off at Sullivan the moment they were introduced:

"I'm very glad to have the pleasure of meeting you, Mr. Sullivan, for you will be able to decide a question which has just arisen between my friend Fred Clay and myself. I maintain that if a composer has a musical theme to express, he can express it as perfectly upon the simple tetrachord of Mercury, in which (as I need not tell you) there are no diatonic intervals at all, as upon the much more complicated dis-diapason (with the four tetrachords and the redundant note), which embraces in its perfect consonance all the simple, double and inverted chords."

Sullivan, though somewhat taken aback, appeared to be impressed.

"Will you oblige me by repeating that question?" he asked.

Gilbert's repetition was word-perfect.

"Well," said Sullivan, "that's a very nice point you have raised. But I fear I cannot answer it offhand. I should like to think it over before giving a definite reply."

He must have thought it over for about thirty years, because Gilbert had not received an answer when Sullivan died.

CHAPTER II

SULLIVAN

I

THE two men who had thus been brought together were radically dissimilar in upbringing, outlook and temperament; their characters were antipathetic and complementary. Friendship between them was out of the question from the start, though if Sullivan had been a woman they would have made a most successful marriage. A union of hearts being impossible, the alternative was a union of arts, and the result was the most successful marriage in history. A symbol of their difference may be found in their respective attitudes to their second Christian names, which they both dropped. William Gilbert disliked "Schwenck," but liked the initials "W.S.G." Arthur Sullivan liked "Seymour," but disliked the initials "A.S.S." On the other hand, this might be instanced as the only point on which they would have agreed if each had been born and christened with the other's names. The question need not detain us.

Sullivan's early years were spent in poverty, and

if, like Gilbert, he had been captured by brigands, his parents could not have ransomed him for twenty-five pounds without selling up the home. His father, an Irishman named Thomas Sullivan, received a guinea a week for playing the clarionette in the orchestra at the Surrey Theatre, adding slightly to this salary by teaching and copying music. Thomas married Maria Clementina Coghlan, a penniless girl of Italian origin, and it is reported that when they first met she was accompanying an organ-grinder and a monkey through the streets of South London. It has also been stated that their son Arthur was partly Jewish by descent, and though this point has never been satisfactorily settled there is no doubt that he displayed certain marked Semitic qualities.

Thomas and his wife lived in a very small house at No. 8 Bolwell Terrace, Lambeth, and when their first son Frederic was born Mrs. Sullivan had to increase their meagre means by putting the baby out to nurse and taking the job of a governess. After a while things began to improve; Thomas got more teaching to do; and as soon as he could afford it his wife returned home, where, on May the 13th, 1842, she gave birth to a second son, Arthur. Three years later Thomas Sullivan became bandmaster at the Royal Military College, and though the pay was so poor that the strictest economy had to be exercised in the home, the appointment was, in his own words, "like the coming of a new day."

An enthusiastic musician, he hoped that one or other of his sons would reveal a gift in the same field, and throughout their early childhood he did all in his power to implant in them a love of music. But as time went on and his financial position showed no signs of improvement, he decided that further encouragement along those lines was profitless, and sent them to school in the hope that they would learn something useful. Arthur went to a private school in Bayswater and quickly showed that he had no use for anything but music. Already he could play every wind instrument in his father's band at Sandhurst, and in later life he declared that from the age of five music was the only thing in the world for which he had cared. When he was eight he composed his first anthem, and two years later, during his first term at school, his mind was greatly exercised over the problem of purchasing a piano on the hire system.

The mere act of acquiring something struck him as an unusually interesting proceeding, and before the piano came into his life he had been with his mother to an auction at Frimley, where, left alone for a while, he had watched a number of people nodding their heads and saying "sixpence." His imagination was fired, and before long he too was nodding his head and saying "sixpence." In this manner a pair of leather hunting-breeches and a flat candlestick with a pair of snuffers passed into his possession, and he was briskly bidding for a sofa when his mother caught sight of him, heard what he had done, and had to explain the position to the auctioneer.

Before he had been a year at school Sullivan's ambition crystallised, and his letters home were full of requests that he might become a chorister in the Chapel Royal. His father tried to divert this desire by encouraging a momentary interest in chemistry, but the letters became so urgent that parental permission was at length obtained. Young Sullivan (now aged twelve) was taken by his schoolmaster to see Sir George Smart, organist of the Chapel Royal, who patted the lad on the head and said that he must call on the Rev. Thomas Helmore, Master of the Chapel Royal. Off they went to Chelsea, and though Mr. Helmore had made a rule that no boy above nine years of age should be admitted to the choir, he took such a fancy to Sullivan that he agreed to give him a trial. Years afterwards Helmore said that he had been impressed, not only by Sullivan's enthusiasm and the beauty of his voice, but chiefly by his knowledge of music. We may doubt this, since people like to claim previsional powers, and beauty of voice is more to be desired in a chorister than a wide knowledge of music. With our fuller knowledge of Sullivan, who had something feminine and appealing about him, we shall not be far wrong if we attribute his success with Helmore to personal charm, not technical equipment.

Sullivan entered the choir of the Chapel Royal and became a pupil in Helmore's school at No. 6 Cheyne Walk in the spring of 1854. Helmore believed in the wisdom of Solomon and implanted knowledge with the aid of a stick. Sullivan's charm did not soften the master's heart, and since he could not be caned, as another boy was, for not knowing the meaning of *fortissimo*, he earned his stripes by a want of interest in Latin and Euclid. While his singing could move the master to tears, his construing aroused a different emotion in Helmore, and the pupil was moved to tears. Worse still, he "had the Gospel to write out ten times for not knowing it," though in his letter home recording the fact he did not specify the evangelist.

Sullivan was a delicate boy, and if he had not lived in a state of exaltation about music it is doubtful whether he would have survived the hard life, the arithmetic and the rod. Twice on Sundays and Saints' Days he had to walk the distance between Chelsea and St. James's Palace, dressed in a heavy, scarlet, gold-braided coat, and the journey tired him so much that on returning to Cheyne Walk he had to lie down to recover. The uniforms of the choristers irritated the less gaudily-dressed street boys, who jeered at them and sometimes pelted them with stones. Once they were violently assailed by a crowd of urchins near Buckingham Palace and might have been severely handled in spite of their desperate defence if a man had not taken their part. Sullivan's comment, "I managed to get home safely," rather suggests that he left the honour of the choir in more capable hands and took to his heels.

Helmore believed in an all-round education and would not allow any of his pupils to concentrate on music. Indeed, he seems to have forced the boys to take an interest in the outside world as well as their studies, for he read them *The Times* account of the Battle of the Alma and the tears rolled down his cheeks when he came to the passages which recounted the heroic deeds of the British soldiers, the tears of his pupils rolling in sympathy. He did not know that Sullivan composed madrigals in bed at night "in deadly fear lest Helmore should come in and catch me," and his clerical dignity would have been seriously upset if he had caught the youngster sitting on the staircase in the dark, long after the other boys had gone to bed, dreaming about Jenny Lind's voice and lost in a state of enchantment.

2

This early training in the choir of the Chapel
Royal had a lifelong influence on Sullivan as an
artist, for even his lighter music has a psalmodic
or hymnic quality, which partly accounts for its
extraordinary popularity among English-speaking
peoples. In effect, too, Sullivan the choir-boy was
Sullivan the national composer. A gentle feminine
appeal to both sexes was his outstanding characteristic as boy and man, and the resultant popularity
helped him at first, though it harmed him at last.
Everyone was nice to him from the start, not only
because of his winning manners and sympathetic
voice, but because he was "such a good boy," so
desirous to please, so anxious to improve. He
brought out the protective instinct in people, who
longed to do things for him, to help him, to look
after him. Women wanted to pet him, men to pat
him. The Bishop of London heard him sing and
tipped him half-a-crown. The iron heart of the
Duke of Wellington was melted to the tune of
half-a-guinea. Another military gentleman listened
to a performance of *Judas* at Battersea and was so
much moved that he proposed three cheers for the
choristers, "especially the one with the black hair."
Maiden ladies, their hearts a-flutter with affection,
would ask and obtain permission to take him in
their carriage to the afternoon service at St. Paul's

Cathedral. At the christening of the Duke of Albany he was chosen to sing a solo in the anthem composed by Michael Costa, who, though delighted with Sullivan's voice, felt that his pronunciation of the words lacked clarity. Costa explained exactly how the words should be accented by singing them himself: "Soofer leetle cheeldren to kom onto me, and forbeed them not, for of sooch is the Keengdom of Haven." Upon reflection, Sullivan decided to retain the authorised version, which pleased Queen Victoria and earned the Prince Consort's congratulations, plus a half-sovereign tip. In addition to all this, he was extremely popular among his fellow-choristers, who appointed him leader of their orchestra, which consisted of a piano, several combs covered with paper, and the cover of a book for a drum.

In the intervals of being praised by princes and spoilt by spinsters Sullivan was working very hard, sometimes refusing to join picnic-parties in order that he might compose anthems. Already he had become a critic of other men's work and described a composition of Rubinstein as "a disgrace to the Philharmonic." His preferences were equally strong, and he was so deeply impressed by a march in *The Martyrdom of St. Polycarp* that he wrote it out from memory and sent it to his father as an ideal work for a military band.

His father, now on the staff of Kneller Hall (a

training school for military musicians), was naturally delighted with Arthur's success, and the happiest moment of his life was when his boy won the
Mendelssohn Scholarship. Since there were seven-
teen competitors in the final examination, all of
them older than Arthur, there was some excuse for
the bandmaster's pride. He wept with joy, told
his wife to kiss "the darling little fellow" a thousand
times for him, and begged her to bring him home
for a day or two, as he longed to embrace him.
Sullivan won the Mendelssohn Scholarship at the
age of fourteen, and it gave him a year at the Royal
Academy of Music. Though excited by his success
he checked the display of his emotions, for at first it
seemed too good to be true. Nothing, he knew,
could ever interest him half so much as music, and
already a great career was opening out before him.
A feeling of humility was uppermost when he wrote
to his father: "I may not make a lot of money, but
I shall have music, and that will make up if I
don't."

Still a choir-boy at the Chapel Royal, he worked
hard at the Royal Academy of Music and received
lessons from, among others, Professor (afterwards
Sir William) Sterndale Bennett, with whom he soon
became a favourite pupil. Bennett gave lessons at
his house in Russell Place, and he would often ask
Sullivan to stay for supper when the other students
were dismissed. The older boys envied him, and it

says much for his pleasing and unassuming disposition that he remained popular with them. At the end of the year he tried for the Scholarship again, and the examiners were so pleased with his progress that he was re-elected for another twelve months. By this time he had written a number of songs which touched the heart and opened the purse of the bishop, dean or sub-dean before whom he sang them. Half-sovereign tips were the order of the day, and Sullivan must have entertained a high opinion of the upper clergy.

His progress during the second year was so exceptional that he was regarded as the most promising student at the Academy, and the Mendelssohn Committee decided to send him for a year to the Leipzig Conservatoire. This meant that he would have to learn German, but with Sullivan difficulties vanished as soon as they appeared. The wife of the Committee's Honorary Secretary was only too delighted to be of help, and she offered to give him lessons in German for nothing. He accepted the offer gratefully, and though he hated the language he discovered that it expressed so much of what he felt that he had to admire it. Possibly it expressed the hatred he felt for it.

After re-election as Mendelssohn Scholar for the third year, Sullivan prepared for the journey to Leipzig. He had of course to leave the Chapel

Royal, but as his voice had not broken he could not qualify for the present of sixty pounds from the Queen and a Bible and Prayer-book from the Bishop of London. This was an immutable law: no broken voice, no sixty pounds and no Holy Writ. But Sullivan was Sullivan; everyone adored him, and so everyone set to work to circumvent the law. It was decided that as a great singer he should receive sixty pounds from the Privy Purse, and it was further decided that as a great singer he was entitled to copies of the sacred texts from the episcopal hands.

3

Sullivan arrived at Leipzig in the autumn of 1858, when the prestige of the Conservatoire in the world of music was at its height. Ignez Moscheles was the chief personality of the place, and he had an enormous reputation throughout Europe. His career as a conductor had been one of sensations. Paris had gone mad about him, London had raved over his performance of Beethoven's Ninth Symphony; Germany, Austria and Holland echoed with praises of his concerts. When Mendelssohn was fifteen Moscheles had taught him harmony, and after Mendelssohn's death Moscheles reigned in his stead at the Leipzig Conservatoire, now championing Schumann with the enthusiasm he had previously reserved for Mendelssohn. Among the professors who served under him at Leipzig were Hauptmann, Richter, Rietz, David and Plaidy.

At first Sullivan wished to become a master of the pianoforte; he had no thoughts of being a composer, but believed he might achieve a position as pianist in London second to none. After a few months this ambition was replaced by another, and he longed above all things to be a great conductor. Later he realised that he had to reveal himself in a more personal way and turned to composition. These are the usual steps of the born artist: first the actor, then the producer, finally the writer; or, less concretely, assertion, expansion, creation.

Sullivan was extremely poor and had to look carefully at every penny (or rather groschen) that he spent. He lived with an English friend, and in this way managed to economise over fires and light, and as he was frequently asked out to supper he was able to keep down his expenses to a minimum. Every month he forwarded a full account of the sums he had spent to his father, who with great difficulty managed to pay his living expenses. So anxious was he not to put a greater burden on his father that, towards the end of the year, he went for afternoon walks with the professors in his dress-suit because his everyday coat was threadbare. His shabbiness did not, however, interfere with his popularity. The professors were delighted to hear him speak so well of his English teachers, for they knew that when he returned home he would speak equally well of themselves. Though people like listening to the criticism of others, they do not like the critic; they feel safer with a dullard who praises. But Sullivan was not a dullard. He was an extremely charming companion, and praise sounded sweet from his lips. He could ingratiate himself with almost anyone. Anxious to be liked and to make a good impression, he always succeeded. Bright, obliging, sincere, no one could resist him. When distinguished visitors came to the Leipzig concerts he invariably contrived to be near at hand and to do some little service which might bring him to their favourable notice. By such means he obtained personal contact with celebrities whom less thoughtful students worshipped at a respectful distance. In later years the possession of this social instinct had much to do with his popularity in Court circles.

His air of deference in the presence of seniors and social superiors was, in view of his obvious accomplishments, one of his most attractive assets, as it was certainly one of the most valuable. People went out of their way to do him good turns, for he was not the kind of man who would scorn the ladder "by which he did ascend." Self-assured and perfectly at ease, he managed to convey the impression that he felt at home wherever he went. When he entered a room full of strangers at Leipzig it was as if he had found himself among a company of old friends; his bearing was so easy, his manner so unconstrained, that an observer would have thought he had been among these folk all his life.

With women his appeal was immediate and often permanent. His oval, olive-tinted face, his dark luminous eyes, his large sensuous mouth, and the generous crop of black curly hair which overhung his low forehead, no doubt added to the attraction. The girls at Leipzig fell in love with him at sight. His appearance aroused strange emotions. "Something happened within me, I knew not what!" exclaimed one of them. And there was much heart-burning and jealousy. Nothing of note seems to have "happened within" Sullivan at the sight of the Leipzig ladies, though he was too amiable not to flirt with the more attractive ones.

He was born under a lucky star, for not only was he admired and helped by others at every stage of his career, but the help always arrived at the very moment when he needed it. A trivial but typical incident occurred in the Leipzig days during a brief holiday that he spent with a friend. They went to Schandau, put up at a hotel, and at the end of a week discovered to their dismay that after paying the bill they would not have enough money for their return journey. While viewing the Royal

c

Palace and wondering what they could do, Sullivan received a dig in the back, looked round, and a second later was greeting an acquaintance, who of course provided the necessary cash.

Shortly after this episode he heard that the Mendelssohn Committee had renewed his Scholarship for another year, in gratitude for which he sat down and composed an anthem, which he dedicated and sent to Sir George Smart, head of the Committee, who had helped and encouraged Sullivan from the moment that he had patted the lad's head five years before. Smart appreciated the compliment and did his best to deserve it by offering to pay five pounds towards the composer's living expenses a year later.

During his second year at the Conservatoire Sullivan began to compose in good earnest. His works served a double purpose: they were good practice for him, and, since he was still hard-up, they made acceptable Christmas and birthday presents for his friends. In June, 1860, his Overture to a poem by Thomas Moore was performed at a students' concert and received with enthusiasm. "It was such fun standing up there and conducting that large orchestra," he wrote to his father: "I can fancy Mother saying now: 'Bless his little heart! how it must have beaten!' But his little heart did not beat at all. I wasn't the least nervous. . . ." His letters home were full of Schumann, then the little god of musical highbrows. Like all the gods of all the highbrows in history, Schumann has had to leave his place in the sun; but there is some excuse for Sullivan's adulation when we remember that England would hardly listen to any music that was not by Handel or Mendelssohn or Chopin for half a century. London's leading musical critic, H. F. Chorley, actually refused to sit in a drawing-room while Schumann's works were being played, retiring to the hall where he sulked until the pianist had the good taste to revert to Mendelssohn.

The music of Schumann, the playing of Joachim, the encouragement of his professors and his early struggles with harmony and counterpoint did not absorb the whole of Sullivan's attention. He loved to wander about Leipzig and the neighbouring country. The German mode of life, the people themselves, and the endless talks on music with his fellow-students, pleased him infinitely. He wondered how such a peaceful, joy-loving race could endure to be herded into ranks of drilling soldiers, and the only inharmonious notes in that smiling landscape were the columns of warriors trailing east and west on the business of the politicians. He came to the conclusion that war and revolution were the result of unemployment. His personal popularity was costly; he was appointed organiser of picnics and such-like distractions, and in many ways had to repay admiration with self-sacrifice.

His second year at Leipzig was drawing to a close when, in August, 1860, nature provided him with one of the themes for his most famous piece of incidental music. The greatest recorded storm in the history of Germany swept over the city. One Monday evening, when Sullivan was out walking with some friends, the clouds began to gather, the air to thicken, the distant moan of the wind was heard, a few large drops of rain fell, and then, suddenly, the atmosphere seemed to explode. Sullivan and his friends witnessed the rest from the protection of an archway. Black night descended, the wind roared and shrieked, chimney-pots fell, tiles crashed, windows smashed, thunder rent the air, lightning hissed, trees toppled, women and children screamed. The hailstones, said Sullivan, were the size of hens' eggs (bantams' probably), and after the storm the streets looked like rivers of broken ice. The damage to man, beast and property was considerable. Sullivan's place was flooded out; he had to take refuge elsewhere for a few days, while the masons and glaziers did a record trade, and before the end of the year he was composing music to Shakespeare's play, *The Tempest*.

Two of the professors, Moscheles and Plaidy, were much concerned over Sullivan's departure and persuaded him to make every effort to stay on at the Conservatoire until the following Easter, as his execution would then be greatly improved and he would be able to play in the Grand Public Examination. Sullivan, knowing that a further extension of his Scholarship was out of the question, wrote to Sir George Smart, who offered to contribute five pounds towards his expenses if he could obtain elsewhere the remaining thirty-five pounds necessary to keep him at Leipzig till Easter. Sullivan then wrote to his father, who had just managed to increase his income by taking classes at Broadwoods, the piano manufacturers, where he gave instruction four nights a week. Somehow Thomas Sullivan managed to raise the requisite sum, and Arthur, transported with gratitude, acknowledged it wholeheartedly: "I will try," said he, "to make the end of your days happy and comfortable." The authorities at the Conservatoire also came up to the scratch and he was exempted from the payment of fees for the remaining six months of his stay. He went to thank the Director, who remarked: "You are a splendid fellow and very useful. We all like you so much that we can't let you go."

After this Sullivan set to work on *The Tempest*, warning his father that he would find the music harsh and unusual at first, but comforting him with the assurance that he might like it when he became accustomed to it. The work was performed at the Grand Public Examination and the com-

poser was called forward three times to acknowledge
the applause. Having obtained an introduction to
Liszt, whom he found very amiable and with whom
he played whist, Sullivan left Leipzig amid tears
and sighs, his hand nearly wrenched off, his coat
almost hugged off, breathless, happy and sorry.

Arrived in England, one of his first visits was to
Sir George Smart, who was delighted to hear that
during his two and a half years' residence abroad
Sullivan had never once been to a concert on
Sunday. Apart from the hint of disapproval
implicit in this self-denial, Sullivan had nothing
but praise for his German friends.

4

On his return to England he found that musical
taste had remained stationary; from the throne to
the home it was still Mendelssohnian. No one
seemed to have heard of Schumann or Schubert,
so he determined to make them known. His first
convert was Cipriani Potter, who controlled the
Royal Academy of Music. His second was George
Grove, Secretary of the Crystal Palace. Grove was
struck by the eager face of an "engaging young
man" who was watching him through the glass
panel of a door during a concert at St. James's Hall
and wished to be introduced to this new and
attractive disciple. Sullivan was quick to take

advantage of such a valuable introduction, and
before long they were great friends, their friendship
being responsible for the popularity of Schumann
and Schubert in England, and also for the early
reputation of Sullivan.

Almost at once Grove appointed him Professor
of Pianoforte and Ballad Singing at the Crystal
Palace School of Art, and this gave Sullivan time
to revise his music to Shakespeare's play. Only
the works of the greatest composers were then being
performed at the Crystal Palace, but Grove made
an exception in the case of Sullivan, and *The
Tempest* appeared in the programme on April 5th,
1862. Like Byron, he awoke next morning to find
himself famous. Such was the success of the music
that it was repeated a few days later (an unprece-
dented occurrence) when London assembled "her
beauty and her chivalry" at Sydenham to enjoy the
latest sensation. After the performance Charles
Dickens rushed round to see the composer, seized
his hand in an iron grip and said: "I don't pretend
to know much about music, but I do know I have
been listening to a very great work." Chorley,
critic of *The Athenæum* and England's chief spokes-
man on musical taste, accompanied Dickens and
was equally enthusiastic, though he of course
knew everything it was tasteful to know about music.
The result was inevitable. Chorley was soon writing
a libretto for Sullivan—a shockingly bad one, but

much must be forgiven an arbiter on taste—and Dickens introduced Sullivan to circles of undoubted worth. Later that year all three visited Paris together, where they heard Gluck's *Orfeo*, the tears streaming down their faces in unison, and where Dickens "rushed about tremendously all the time," talking excitedly to cabmen in very bad French, dining at all sorts of restaurants and calling on all sorts of people. Sullivan was even more impressed by Dickens's personality than by his novels, and the visit was a great success. They saw the ageing Rossini, who took an instant fancy to Sullivan, called him *"mon jeune collègue,"* played duets from *The Tempest* with him, and begged him to write regularly and to send copies of everything he composed.

Sullivan's future was now assured. *The Tempest* was the talk of musical London (after the compositions of Handel and Mendelssohn), and since teaching was uncongenial to him, he obtained the post of organist at St. Michael's, Chester Square, which gave him enough to live on while he was composing. His choir caused him some trouble at first. There were women in abundance, but he was short of men. However, a police-station was situated nearby, and having made friends with the Chief Superintendent, he recruited his tenors and basses from the force. They were a little dull in the opening stages of instruction.

"Now, my men," Sullivan would say, striking a chord, "what key is this in?"

No response. The force refused to be caught.

"Don't all speak at once. One at a time, if you please."

"B, sir," volunteered a shy tenor, possibly because his number was B 47.

"Major or minor?"

"Minor, sir," with greater confidence.

The rest looked approvingly at B 47 for having vindicated the honour of the force.

"No, that won't do," said Sullivan.

The force looked suspiciously first at the organist and then at B 47, wondering which of the two was making a fool of them.

"It is G minor," said Sullivan.

That seemed to settle the question. There was a deep sigh from the force and glances of sympathy and relief passed from one to the other.

In time Sullivan managed to produce one of the best choirs in London. Then he doubled his duties and went to St. Peter's, Cranley Gardens, finally closing his career as an organist in 1872.

Apart from these religious exercises, composing did not occupy the whole of his time. There were a number of small choral societies which met and sang in private houses, and by joining one or two of these he became acquainted with the more notable figures in society and public life. He met

C*

Gladstone, and one evening at Carlton House Terrace he sang with the famous orator from the same copy. He also met Disraeli, who asked him to explain the process of musical composition. After his explanation Disraeli said: "Well, it is still a wonder to me, but you have made many things much clearer to me than they were before." Curiously enough, Gladstone asked him the same question, but before six words were out of his mouth the Prime Minister interrupted him and gave an eloquent discourse on the subject. Sullivan preferred Disraeli.

Throughtout the 'sixties he lived in Pimlico, first at No. 3 Ponsonby Street, then in a house on the south side of Lupus Street, finally with his parents at No. 47 Claverton Terrace; and all the time he was producing songs, of which *Orpheus With His Lute*, *O Mistress Mine* and *The Willow Song* are still well known. At the start he sold them outright for five or ten guineas apiece, but finding that the publishers were making large sums out of them, he determined to sell them on a royalty basis. In this way his income was considerably augmented, while his *Tempest* music, which Grove repeatedly performed at the Crystal Palace, was spreading his reputation abroad in the land. He became something of a social lion, and though he basked in the universal admiration, he recognised its absurdity. "I stood about the room in easy and graceful postures, conscious of being gazed upon," he wrote from Manchester, where he was present at the first performance of *The Tempest* and where he was "taken to a ball and shown about like a stuffed gorilla."

His friends at this period were mostly drawn from the world of music, chief among them being the Groves, the Lehmanns, Jenny Lind and Fred Clay. His twenty-first birthday was spent with the Lehmanns in the " delirious dullness of Madame Tussaud's" and he frequently travelled abroad with them during the next twenty-five years. Fred Clay had followed Sullivan at Leipzig; he was a thorough bohemian, easy-going, genial, living only for the day; he went everywhere and knew everyone; turning out his songs by the dozen, selling them for a song, and heedless as to their merit. His output happened to include three of the most popular songs of the age—*The Sands of Dee, She Wandered Down the Mountain Side* and *I'll Sing Thee Songs of Araby*—each of which was sold by him for the sum of five pounds, though after the last-named had made a fortune for the publishers they were generous enough to hand on twenty pounds of it to the composer. Clay, however, did something that more nearly concerns us than any of his songs: he introduced Gilbert to Sullivan, and therefore occupies an important niche in the edifice of Savoy Opera.

Sullivan frequently stayed with George Grove at Sydenham and was soon on a familiar footing with the other directors of the Crystal Palace, among them Scott Russell, with one of whose daughters he fell in love. It was his first serious love-affair, and it inspired a number of songs, two of which echoed through British drawing-rooms for several seasons. Their titles—*O Fair Dove* and *O Fond Dove*—do not perhaps suggest the kind of passion that inspired the love-letters of Keats, and indeed a sentence in the lady's letter of rejection proves that his emotions were always expressed with a strict regard to propriety. "Your young life," she wrote, "shall not be dimmed by the nurture of a hope which will never be fulfilled." Her parents objected to the match, and Sullivan was not the man to set at defiance, in the interests of the heart, a whole Board of Directors. She, too, could not envision a world beyond Sydenham; and so they had to content themselves with a series of sighs, coupled with prayers for strength to endure their lot with humble resignation. The attitude of the parents has never been explained, though its reason may be guessed. Sullivan had a genius for friendship with men who were older and more influential than himself, and this was his first serious check. Obviously there were limits to the friendship on their side. It pleased them to recognise his talents, but not his parents, and they believed that in the sacrament of marriage there was a wide difference between the possession of a respectable genius and the possession of a respectable genealogy.

5

The writing of songs, admirably though they expressed the feelings of his heart, did not occupy all Sullivan's spare time during the years of his courtship. He was ambitious. He wanted to conquer the entire realm of music and naturally he aimed at grand opera. Through the influence of a friend he was allowed to watch the rehearsals at Covent Garden and was eventually appointed organist at the Opera House. This placed him under the direction of the stage-manager, in his dealings with whom Sullivan displayed an almost obsequious deference. He was commissioned to write the music to a ballet, *L'Ile Enchantée*, and the stage-manager asked him to fill up a pause in the performance with a musical passage for the 'cellos. Sullivan looked admiringly at the stage-manager and said: "You have opened up a new path of beauty in orchestration." However, he soon tired of being a musical carpenter, and, having learnt what he wanted to know, he left Covent Garden.

After that a visit to Ireland resulted in a symphony, and then H. F. Chorley handed Sullivan the libretto of the opera on which the famous critic had been working ever since they had met at the Crystal Palace. It was a ghastly production, utterly unsuitable for stage or music, but Chorley was too important to be told so, and Sullivan wrestled with the incubus. Banking on the successful storm-music Sullivan had already written for *The Tempest*, Chorley had given him another storm in the opera. But it is difficult to ring the changes on storms, and Sullivan, unlike nature, did not care to repeat himself. At length it became apparent even to the librettist that his collaborator was not working with the zest of inspiration; and as the promoters of the Birmingham Festival had just asked Sullivan to write a cantata, he was able to divert Chorley's enthusiasm for storms into less turbulent channels. The critic produced another bad libretto, on which the composer worked feverishly day and night, and in due time *Kenilworth* was produced at Birmingham. To Sullivan's great joy his father witnessed the enthusiasm which greeted the first performance.

The success of an all-Sullivan concert at the Crystal Palace brought an invitation from the Committee of the Norwich Festival to write something for production at the end of October, 1866. Sullivan accepted it, but his inspiration seemed to have dried up, and for weeks he struggled with unsatisfactory themes. His father told him not to worry, as the moment was sure to arrive when the melody for which he was searching would reveal itself and compel expression. The days went by, September came, and still his meditations bore no fruit. Half-mad with anxiety, he had almost abandoned hope when the moment his father had foretold arrived. His father died, and the blow prostrated him. He forgot the Norwich Festival, forgot the subject of his frantic efforts, forgot everything but his sorrow. "My dear, dear Father, whom I loved so passionately," he exclaimed in the anguish of his loss, "Oh, it is so hard—it is so terribly hard—to think that I shall never see his dear face again, or hear his cheery voice saying: 'God bless you, my boy'." He tried to behave calmly in the presence of his distraught mother, to whom he could not bear to speak of their sorrow because he felt so "sick and choky," but when alone he gave himself up to grief: "In great pain of this kind one holds out one's hands in an agony to see if anyone will clutch them and press them even for a moment only." Soon he tried to ease his heartache in work, and since his mind was full of his father the work quickly took shape, becoming *In Memoriam*, which was performed on October 30th, 1866, at the Norwich Festival. It placed him definitely in the front rank of living composers and is still heard more often than any of his longer orchestral pieces.

His tribute to the art of English music being thus acclaimed, Sullivan wished to render service to the art of a great continental master. He and Grove had done much to popularise both Schumann and Schubert in England, but they longed to discover some of the latter's lost music and so to found his reputation more securely. Above all, they wanted to find the missing portions of the *Rosamunde* music. With this object in view they went to Vienna in the autumn of 1867, visiting Madame Schumann and the birthplace of Mozart on the way. Spina, the Viennese music-publisher, received them rapturously, produced piles of manuscripts and shut them into a room with plenty of cigars. For a week they pored over the dusty pages of forgotten composers, and though they found much of interest there was no sign of the work for which they hungered. Spina's clerk, Döppler, had known Beethoven and Schubert, and they listened with amazement while the old man, hardly realising that he had once walked with gods, told anecdotes of life on Olympus. They were introduced to one of Schubert's relations, Dr. Schneider, who produced a deal of musty material from his cupboard, but not what they were looking for. On the last day of their visit they went to take leave of Schneider, who said that he believed he had once had a copy of the *Rosamunde* music. Grove asked whether he could rummage in the cupboard and see for himself. The Doctor assented, but warned him that he would get covered with dust. Grove was hunting for diamonds and did not mind the dust. He entered the cupboard, and after several suffocating minutes emerged with the part books of the entire *Rosamunde* music, which he had found carefully hidden beneath everything else. Delirious with excitement, Sullivan and Grove sat up till two the next morning copying the parts, and concluded their labours with a game of leap-frog.

Having packed an Overture and two Symphonies (C major and C minor) by Schubert in their trunks, together with the complete *Rosamunde*, they returned home via Prague, Leipzig (where Sullivan conducted his *In Memoriam*), Dresden (where he heard Wagner's *Rienzi*, thinking it "very commonplace, vulgar and uninteresting") and Paris.

His reputation as a writer of songs was now considerable. Robert Browning had a friend to whose poems he begged Sullivan to write music, and even Alfred Tennyson flirted with the idea of a collaboration with the fashionable composer. Browning's protégé did not appeal to Sullivan, but Tennyson did, and he went to stay with the Poet Laureate, who read aloud his twelve Songs of the Wrens. Sullivan was enchanted and did his utmost to persuade Tennyson to let him set them to music. Though professing to think that they might lessen his reputation, the Laureate agreed on condition that Millais should illustrate them. Sullivan began to work on them at once and had almost finished his part of the job when Tennyson became the prey of compunction. Perhaps one or two friends had said that the songs did not require music, that they sang themselves, that any composer but their author would vulgarise them. Perhaps (though this is improbable) the poet really did think they were unworthy of him. At any rate his attitude became increasingly dilatory and harassing, and at last Millais retired from the project in a fit of petulance.

Sullivan persisted grimly; so grimly indeed that Tennyson, realising that the matter had passed beyond the dallying stage, offered the composer five hundred pounds to drop the scheme. The discussion raged for three years, when the Franco-German war furnished Tennyson with another excuse. Such trifles, said he, must not be published at such a grave crisis in European affairs; it was scarcely a moment for a national poet to appear flippant. But Sullivan wished to link his name with the Laureate's and saw nothing essentially incongruous in war and flippancy. Tennyson had to give way, but he insisted on writing an introduction in which he explained that at the composer's request he had dressed up "a puppet in the old style, a mere motif for an air, indeed the veriest nothing unless Mr. Sullivan can make it dance to his instruments." He also implied that, but for his promise, he would not have made his puppet dance at all "in the dark shadow of these days."

Sullivan did not relish such words, especially as his friends advised him that they amounted to a public insult. He wrote to Tennyson for an explanation, and since the poet did not deign to reply, he continued to write. Tennyson at last gave judgment. He had considered the complaint, had submitted the question to various friends, and in effect had decided that Sullivan had not been insulted. Sullivan, always anxious to look on the bright side of things, appeared to be satisfied. He had indeed a remarkable capacity for not feeling insulted in the most trying circumstances, which was to prove a valuable asset in the days to come.

6

By the dawning of the 'seventies Sullivan had become a figure of note and had produced his first oratorio, *The Prodigal Son;* a sign that he was seriously in the running with Handel and Mendelssohn, who provided the Victorians with a religious reason for liking music. • His personal popularity in social circles was also assured. His sentimental songs paved the way and his personal charm did the rest: he was, as composer and man, the darling of drawing-rooms. No one could possibly object to him, except as a son-in-law, because he had all the arts of making himself pleasant at his tongue's tip. The soft answer that turneth away wrath, the deferential word, the flattering phrase, the interested query, the enthusiastic exclamation, the understanding nod, the look of appeal, the soulful glance, the tactful gesture, the kindly laugh; all were perfectly timed and controlled by an art that was but partly conscious. Naturally lazy and genial, he was born for the salon, and the only criticism ever passed on him was that he had lavished on the salon (some said the Savoy) the gifts that were meant for mankind (some said oratorio).

Above all he was extremely popular with members of royal families; they loved him and he loved them. No famous artist in England has ever received so many marks of royal favour and none has been able to maintain such a loyal passion for the society of princes. From the moment when the Prince Consort tipped him half-a-guinea he never looked back, and the tipping became mutual. They bestowed honours and decorations on him; he wrote marches and Te Deums for them. They asked him to their country-house gatherings; he did his best to join in their pursuits, making a poor shot and an unsteady rider.

He lived on intimate terms with the exiled Napoleon III and the Empress Eugénie and frequently invited their son the Prince Imperial to his house. The King of Denmark, the Czar and Czarina of Russia, the Kaiser and Prince Henry of Prussia, were among his acquaintances and admirers. Queen Victoria asked him for a complete set of his works and even requested him to correct the compositions of the Prince Consort. The Prince and Princess of Wales were devoted to him, and one of his closest friends was the Duke of Edinburgh. A sentence in one of his letters is characteristic. He met Prince Leopold, afterwards Duke of Albany, at Oxford in May, 1873. "We chummed together," Sullivan wrote, "and he gave me his photograph." This catalogue could be extended to include most of the royal or semi-royal persons of the day, but the Almanach de Gotha is available for further reference.

Apart from Sullivan's innate gift for composing light music, one of the causes of his early experiments in comic opera may have been his desire to give the dukes and princes on his visiting list the kind of entertainment they could understand and enjoy; for no sooner had he been acclaimed by grave critics as the chief hope of religious music in England than he started trifling with a giddier muse. One day he met Burnand, who suggested that Sullivan should write the music to a burlesque he had written for an amateur company. Though asked to do it for nothing, Sullivan agreed, and to his amazement the little piece, *Cox and Box*, became popular, making a lot of money for charitable causes. At that time the German Reeds were providing the more respectable elements in London society with exhibitions of "clean fun," in order to counteract the coarseness of the burlesques that were then the rage. The Reeds discovered that there was a lot of money in clean fun, and they became ambitious; from a piano and sketches they went on to an orchestra and operas; and when Burnand and Sullivan offered them an ambitious comic opera called *The Contrabandista* they jumped at it. Unfortunately it was a complete failure, and in despair Sullivan returned to more serious composition. Songs and religious music began to pour from him again and he travelled all over the country conducting his works.

Then came his introduction to Gilbert, and within a year they were working together on an operatic Extravaganza entitled *Thespis*, which John Hollingshead produced at the Gaiety Theatre on December 23rd, 1871. Sullivan was delighted with the way in which Gilbert produced this piece, making the chorus an essential part of the action instead of the usual singing "turn," and also with his handling of the artists. "Really, Mr. Gilbert, why should I stand here? I am not a chorus-girl!" exclaimed one of the principals indignantly. "No, madam," returned Gilbert, "your voice is not strong enough, or no doubt you would be."

In spite of Gilbert's efforts *Thespis* was not a
success. It ran for a month and the collaborators
separated, one to write more blank-verse plays,
the other to set hymns and to fall in love again.
This time it was with an Irishwoman, who incited
him to vie with Handel and Mendelssohn and who
was partly responsible for his next oratorio. The
facts of the affair have not been disclosed. We only
know that he visited Ireland again and again. that
his love found expression in *The Light of the World*,
and that in time he ceased to visit Ireland. The
oratorio was produced at Birmingham in 1873,
and the Duke of Edinburgh was so overcome by
the performance that he went on repeating the
words "A triumph!" until it occurred to him that
the fact was established. Gounod pronounced the
work a masterpiece and Queen Victoria believed
it was "destined to uplift British music."

Rumours began to fly about that Sullivan was
to be knighted. He had almost snatched the laurels
from Mendelssohn, and had already given the
Church of England its most rousing martial tune.
It was fairly generally felt that a knighthood would
be worthily bestowed on the composer of *Onward
Christian Soldiers*.

CHAPTER III

I

ONE day, early in the year 1875, the manager of the Royalty Theatre, Soho, happened to meet Gilbert in the street. The manager's name was Richard D'Oyly Carte, and the fact that he was known to certain members of the theatrical profession as "Oily Carte" implies that his success was partly due to his manner. But manners are not everything, and his success was primarily due to a genius for spotting "winners" which the rest of the world still regarded as "outsiders." When he met Gilbert in the year 1875 he had already perceived that a combination of Gilbert and Sullivan would probably make a fortune for anyone with gumption enough to back them, and he asked the dramatist whether he would write a one-act piece for music by Sullivan to fill the bill at the Royalty, where Offenbach's *La Perichole* was shortly to be produced. Curiously enough, Gilbert had recently dramatised a story he had written for *Fun* and Carl Rosa had agreed to do the music for it; but the death of Mrs. Rosa had resulted in the return of the libretto, and Gilbert promised to let Carte read it. Carte immediately saw its possibilities and arranged a meeting between Gilbert and Sullivan.

On a bitterly cold morning, the snow falling thickly, Gilbert donned a heavy fur coat, stuffed the manuscript of *Trial by Jury* into one of its pockets and called on Sullivan. Whether the cold had got into his bones, or he was suffering from the disappointment frequently felt by an author over an earlier work written in a frame of mind he cannot recapture, it is impossible to say. At any rate, he gave Sullivan the impression that he thought the piece beneath his genius, reading it with growing indignation, his manner becoming more flustered and furious as he proceeded, and finishing the business with a violent gesture and a hostile snort. Meanwhile Sullivan had been rocking with silent laughter from beginning to end of the recital. The libretto was exactly suited to his taste, and within a fortnight he had set it to music. It was produced at the Royalty Theatre on March 25th, 1875, and made such a sensation that, though played as an after-piece, it quickly became the main attraction. Sullivan's brother, Frederic, was so good as the Judge that Gilbert attributed the success of the piece "in no slight degree" to his performance; while W. S. Penley, afterwards famous in *Charley's Aunt* and *The Private Secretary*, made his first appearance on the stage as the Foreman of the Jury.

D'Oyly Carte was not content to see his "outsiders" romp home in one race. Moreover, he was ambitious; he wished to be an owner, not merely a backer. But he was a cautious man; he did not care to risk all until he was sure of winning all; so he decided to form a company. After assuring Gilbert and Sullivan that their future was safe in his keeping and obtaining their assurance that they would not work together for anyone else, he began the search for money. His efforts were not successful at first, because no one believed there was any money to be made out of English light opera. *Trial by Jury*, said the people with fat purses, was a flash in the pan. Could the authors fill the bill? Could they succeed with a full-length opera? That was the question. Carte believed they could, and as he had not been a theatrical agent for nothing, he managed at length to persuade certain music-publishers that the game was worth a gamble.

In his day and in his way Carte was a remarkable person. Born in 1844, he had started life in his father's business as a musical instrument-maker. But the theatre attracted him, and at an early age he began to write songs and operettas. Then he ran a musical and dramatic agency, which quickly became the most successful in London. He varied the booking of tours for "stars" and companies with the management of London theatres; and when he brought Gilbert and Sullivan together for the second time he was about the best-known "middleman" in the profession. This position had been achieved by his skill in the rapid diagnosis of business and professional qualities in the people he met. He regarded human beings as so many subjects for exploitation. He wished to be a Napoleon in the world of the theatre, and the inhabitants of that world were thus potential recruits for his army. In order to assess their value with accuracy it was necessary to be on good terms with them, and with his main object always in view he commenced life as a bon vivant, a jolly good fellow, whose sole object appeared to be the enjoyment of a pleasant, easy, happy-go-lucky existence. In this way he gained a familiar footing in certain useful circles, inviting and receiving confidences which gave him considerable knowledge of movements that were going on behind the scenes. His conversational style was tinged with a humorous and worldly irony, which his acquaintances found attractive and which gave him a certain standing as one "in the know" and therefore one who should be known. He possessed also a rare talent for detail; nothing was too slight or too insignificant for his notice; he took as much care over the pence as he did over the pounds.

When he became rich he was generous with his

money (a typical Napoleonic gesture), but not a few of the actors who had worked for him considered that they were the real benefactors when they learnt that he had left a quarter of a million pounds at his death. George Grossmith, one of his victims, wrote an account of Carte's methods which paints the astute manager to the life. When Grossmith was asked to appear in *The Sorcerer* he told Carte that he was taking a considerable risk, as the Y.M.C.A. would never again engage him as an entertainer after he had once been seen on the stage and his reputation as a comic singer to religious communities would be lost from the moment he performed in a theatre. Carte, whose sole concern was to get Grossmith for three guineas a week less than he had asked, suggested that they should adjourn for lunch and talk it over. After an excellent meal of oysters and wine Grossmith was in a yielding mood and Carte persuaded him to waive the extra three guineas a week. On leaving the Savoy eleven years later Grossmith said that, irrespective of accumulative interest, that lunch had cost him about eighteen hundred pounds. Carte got another actor, Arthur Law, to sign a contract in which he was to understudy a leading part, play old men, women, juveniles or anything he might be cast for, and write curtain-raisers when required, all for about two pounds a week. Many cases of a similar nature have been reported, but

Grossmith's story tells us all we need to know about that aspect of the man, which we shall have to keep in sight when we reach the crisis of the famous Savoy partnership.

The partnership was slow in forming. By the close of 1876 Carte had decided to float a company with himself as managing director. This was known as the Comedy Opera Company, and it was financed by Carte and four others, two of whom, Chappell and Metzler, were music publishers. The Company took a lease of the Opera Comique in Wych Street, Strand, and by the middle of 1877 they were ready to produce the next opera by Gilbert and Sullivan.

2

But Gilbert and Sullivan were not yet ready with their opera. Gilbert had by no means decided that libretti were his strong suit; his heart still hankered after "straight" plays; and before he started working on his next opera he wrote and produced a drama, *Dan'l Druce*, and a farce, *Engaged*. Sullivan was in the same boat. His musical friends were perturbed by his sudden success in light opera and did their best to keep his thoughts from wandering in such facile fields. Two of them, Sir Coutts and Lady Lindsay, took him off to Italy in the summer of 1875, in the hope that, brooding on Lake Como, his mind would turn to higher issues. But the soft air of the place made him lazy, and it was impossible to think of oratorios when the sun was shining or when the still water gave back the moon's reflection, and the mountains stood around like guardian ghosts, and the lights of the villages twinkled in the distance, and the sound of mandolines came from the boats that specked the glassy surface of the lake.

Prone to laziness, he was always fighting it by the formation of sudden resolutions, which he carried into effect before he had time to regret them. He left Como at a moment's notice and returned to London, staying a few hours at Cologne on the way, where he went to the cathedral and "burst out crying, as I always do at children's voices." At home again he plunged into work, writing songs—among them *Thou'rt Passing Hence*, which sobbed its way through the concert-halls of England for two decades—and conducting orchestras up and down the country.

He was a creature of extremes; his periods of absolute idleness were succeeded by periods of feverish occupation; he completely abandoned himself either to a condition of mental vacuum or to one of mental vigour; there was no half-way house for him. Two of the reasons for these excesses of restlessness and inertia may be inferred from his physical health and his spiritual being. From 1872 to the end of his life he was subject to agonising spasms of pain due to stone in the kidney; the presence or near-presence of this disease drove him to work in a frantic effort to forget it; its complete absence was such a relief that he would take advantage of the blessed interregnum and revel in the futilities of social life or dream away the hours in some rural retreat. The spiritual aspect is rather more complicated. He was secretly discontented with the serious work that he had already done, that he felt he ought to go on doing, that his friends were always begging him to do, and therefore a little ashamed of the fact that the lighter type of composition came to him with such frightening facility. It was the old story once again of the natural comedian who wanted to play Hamlet. Further, he was not altogether happy in the temperament that impelled him into social circles which had no proper contact with the world of music to which he truly belonged, which could only distract him from his creative purpose, use him for their own amusement and give him nothing in exchange but excitement and the illusion of fame. From his illness, and from his inner dissatisfaction with his musical gifts and social popularity, he was in ceaseless retreat, and he tried to drug the physical pain and soothe the spiritual discomfort with bouts of activity that left no time for thought and fits of indolence that excluded thought.

Though each agreed in under-estimating the work he did in collaboration with the other, the attitude of Sullivan to his serious compositions was quite different from that of Gilbert to his serious plays, and herein lay their essential difference of character. Gilbert had an extremely high opinion of his contribution to what he believed to be the higher drama, and while Sullivan turned to comic opera with relief Gilbert turned to it with regret. Any internal discomfort over his work that Gilbert endured was due, not to a feeling that he could not live up to his best, but to a feeling that the general public could not live up to his best. Thus he had no need to forget himself in a constant social whirl or in a sort of negative dreamland. His irritation with the world for its lack of appreciation was expressed in irruptions of wit or explosions of temper, while his laziness was that of a healthy man, not a lapse into coma but a deepening of self-consciousness.

It was because Gilbert did not wish to stop writing "straight" plays that over two and a half years elapsed before *Trial by Jury* was followed by another joint-production, and during that interval several things of importance happened to Sullivan. The Duke of Edinburgh, seconded by the Prince of Wales, persuaded him to become Principal of the National Training School of Music, out of which the Royal College of Music was born; and he was

given the honorary degree of Doctor in Music by
the University of Cambridge. These distinctions,
apart from the new duties resulting from the first,
increased the demands on his time as a conductor,
and he hurried from place to place in a vortex of
engagements, spending half his time in cheerless
trains and chilly cabs, and sometimes suffering
so acutely from his disease during a performance
that he could not see the audience for the tears of
agony that streamed from his eyes.

But something that was far more tragic for him
than personal ill-health occurred in January, 1877.
Sullivan's affection for his mother, his father and
his brother, was abnormally strong. Again we note
the difference between him and Gilbert, whose
relations hardly exist for the biographer. But then
Gilbert was a truly typical Englishman, unlike
Dr. Johnson, who, though we like to flatter ourselves into a contrary belief, was no more a typical
Englishman than Voltaire was a typical Frenchman; for men of outstanding genius or personality
cannot be types. Sullivan's feeling for his family
was essentially un-English. It was the feeling of a
stranger in an alien land for his kin. Their very
existence supported him, made life's struggle worth
the pains. Their interests were identical, as the
interests of people in a besieged city are identical.
Though Sullivan could adapt himself to external
circumstances with an ease that was quite beyond
D

the ability, not to say the desire, of Gilbert, yet he was never on an absolutely equal footing with his English contemporaries, and only found complete communion of spirit in his home and among his people. He shared this adaptability, this sense of isolation and this family-feeling with many men of Jewish origin.

When, therefore, his brother Frederic fell ill at the beginning of 1877, Sullivan abandoned everything and spent all his time in the sick-room. Frederic had been his most intimate friend and he loved him as no Englishman loves a brother; that is to say, he would thankfully have died instead. Frederic had been an architect, but he could sing well and had a real talent for comedy, which Sullivan was quick to encourage the moment an opportunity occurred, and since he had made a big hit as the Judge in *Trial by Jury* Gilbert wrote the leading part in their next opera for him. But the fates were against Frederic, whose death at the age of thirty-nine bereft Sullivan of the will to work. For weeks he did nothing and scarcely even saw his friends for fear he should suddenly burst out crying and cause them distress. In the spring of that year the publication of his most famous song, *The Lost Chord*, made an unparalleled sensation. Everyone who could sing, and thousands who couldn't, sang it, and the whole country resounded with its melancholy strains. Sullivan had written it while watching at the bedside of Frederic, and so it became a monody for his brother, just as *In Memoriam* had been a requiem for his father.

The popularity of the tune went beyond reasonable bounds, and as a consequence it was parodied by various people. Whenever he could trace the perpetrator Sullivan wrote and asked that the parody should be suppressed, as the song had been written in great distress at his brother's death; though he lessened the appeal in one instance by adding that "apart from all sentiment, parodies are most damaging to the sale of a song."

3

Meanwhile Gilbert, who never did more work for his money than was absolutely necessary, had been busy turning the material of an early story into the libretto for which Carte was pressing him, and at the beginning of April, 1877, he despatched *The Sorcerer* to Sullivan. Weeks of delay followed. Sullivan had not recovered from his brother's death and the engagement of a suitable cast presented grave difficulties.

Gilbert had experienced so much trouble with leading actors that he decided to have no "stars" in his company, but instead to train a number of amateurs, or at least professional beginners, for the peculiar needs of his operas. He had an especial objection to tenors, who were usually tempera-

mental and liable to walk out of the theatre when
given advice. "They never can act," he declared,
"and they are more trouble than all the other
members of the company put together." At the
end of his life he said that the tenor had been the
curse of every piece he had written. Fortunately
he did not write his leading parts for tenors, and
the directors of the Company were horrified when
they heard that he had engaged a drawing-room
entertainer named George Grossmith, who had
never once appeared on the professional stage, for
the principal part, and a man with an uncertain
ear for music named Rutland Barrington, also quite
inexperienced as an actor, for another important
part. Even Grossmith himself wondered why he
was being engaged for the leading character in a
comic opera.

"I should have thought you required a fine man
with a fine voice," he said.

"No, that is just what we don't want," replied
Gilbert.

Barrington was equally curious about his own
engagement to play the part of a parson, but Gilbert
consoled him with the assurance that as his father
had once very nearly been a clergyman he obviously had the Church in his blood. Asked by someone else why he had taken the risk of casting Barrington for a singing part, Gilbert answered: "He's
a staid, stolid swine, and that's what I want."

As things turned out these were his two most successful pieces of casting. Grossmith and Barrington became inseparable from Savoy Opera and made the hits of their lives in the works of Gilbert and Sullivan. But while Barrington remained immovable and unteachable, depending entirely on his personality, as Gilbert had foreseen, Grossmith's mercurial gifts had to be moulded afresh by Gilbert with each opera. Barrington was the only man who ever spoke Gilbert's words exactly as the author wanted them spoken. Grossmith was the only man who, with a method and personality foreign to Gilbert's requirements, yet contrived by dint of intensive training to recreate the characters in his own image and add something of value to their creator's conception. Grossmith was highly strung and suffered agonies at rehearsals. Barrington was placid and did not know the meaning of nerves. Gilbert understood them both and treated each according to his nature. When Barrington, during the rehearsals of *The Sorcerer*, remarked that it was a daring experiment to introduce a clergyman into comic opera and that the public would either take very kindly to the actor who played the role or hoot him off the stage for ever, Gilbert retorted: "I quite agree with you," and left him wondering. Had Grossmith been rehearsing the part and suffering the same apprehension, Gilbert would have comforted him.

Sullivan put the finishing touches to his music at the beginning of November, 1877, and *The Sorcerer* was produced at the Opera Comique on the 17th of that month. Its career of six months was nearly broken short on several occasions by the nervousness of Carte's fellow-directors, who wanted to close the theatre whenever the booking showed a downward tendency and changed their minds the moment it improved. Gilbert was so pleased with the reception of the piece that he began another at once, while Sullivan's pleasure took the form of a holiday in Paris. He was extremely fond of Paris, and went there whenever he could invent an excuse for the trip. As a further example of his invariable good luck, it may be mentioned that when he visited the French capital in the summer of '77 he happened to meet the chairman of the railway at Victoria Station, who took him as far as Calais in a reserved carriage and cabin at the cost of the company and then managed to get a carriage to themselves on to Paris.

Just before the end of the year Sullivan received the scenario of *H.M.S. Pinafore* from Gilbert, who said: "I have very little doubt whatever but that you will be pleased with it." Sullivan was so much pleased with it that, returning home, he began to work on it at once, in spite of the most violent attacks of illness. Throughout the entire period of composition he was racked with pain, and only managed to complete the work between paroxysms of agony which almost left him insensible.

Paroxysms of a different kind were taking place on the stage during rehearsals. Gilbert was already enforcing those methods of production which were to make his name a byword in the profession and revolutionise the art of dramatic presentation. He had learnt from Robertson that, in drama, the whole was greater than the part, and he was busy subordinating his actors to the play. He regarded each of his libretti as a composer regards a symphony, which can be wrecked by the playing of a single false note, and he determined from the outset to achieve perfect harmony from his orchestra of actors. Every word had to be said with a certain inflection, every movement had to be made in a certain manner, every position had to be judged to a square inch, every piece of "business" had to be considered in its relation to the scene. The actors were not allowed, as in the old days, to emerge for an instant from the frame of the picture he was trying to create. They were like chessmen on a board, to be moved at the discretion of the player-producer; they were like marionettes, whose motions were governed by the master; they were the members of a team, under the strict discipline of its captain.

For this reason he preferred his actors to be novices, who could be taught by himself and would not resent the teaching. For this reason, too, he arrived at the first rehearsal with a fairly complete mental picture of all the moves, all the inflections, all the "business" and all the positions of all the actors at every moment of the play. For hour after hour before the commencement of rehearsals he would sit at his desk with replicas of the scenes on a scale of half an inch to a foot, with blocks of wood three inches high representing the males, two and a half inches high representing the females, and work out every detail of the production. It was not likely therefore that he was going to stand any non-sense from an actor who was solely concerned with his part and who did not mind what happened to the play so long as he made a personal success. At the rehearsals of *Pinafore* a player of the older school refused to repeat for perhaps the fiftieth time a piece of "business" which Gilbert was patiently instructing him to do.

"No, sir, I object," said the actor warmly. "I have been on the stage quite long enough."

"Quite," agreed Gilbert, and dismissed him on the spot.

Gilbert could never see eye-to-eye with people who considered that their proper place was in the centre of the stage, and when a lady who was rehearsing the part of Josephine in *Pinafore* pointed out that she had always occupied that position in Italian Opera, he remarked:

"Unfortunately this is not Italian Opera, but only a low burlesque of the worst possible kind."

The lady continued her career in Italian Opera.

Another well-known actress who was cast for a part in *Pinafore* walked out of the theatre when she heard that a newcomer with no experience named Jessie Bond was to play in her scenes. Though upsetting at the time, it turned out luckily for Gilbert and Sullivan, as Jessie Bond became one of the most popular Savoy favourites.

Explosions between producer and actors were frequent in the early days, though when Gilbert had gained the complete ascendancy over his actors that had always been his aim, their occurrence was rare. His anger only flashed out when anyone questioned his authority, and his wit was usually confined to such harmless squibs as that recorded by Barrington:

"Cross left on that speech, I think, Barrington, and sit on the skylight over the saloon, pensively," advised Gilbert at a rehearsal of *Pinafore*.

The actor did so, but the stage carpenter had sewn the skylight with packthread and it collapsed under Barrington's fourteen stone.

"That's *ex*pensively," remarked Gilbert.

H.M.S. Pinafore was produced on May 25th, 1878, and, its merits apart, caused something of a sensation because of the caricature of W. H. Smith, the publisher, who had recently been

D*

appointed First Lord of the Admiralty by Disraeli.
For some of the lyrics Gilbert had drawn on the
Bab Ballads, one of which he adapted for his present
purpose. This cutting ridicule of the political game,
together with the satire on blatant patriotism in the
same opera, reveals a vital aspect of Gilbert's
character and explains why he had to wait so long
for a knighthood.

It must be repeated that the qualities of wariness
and daring were mixed in his nature in about
equal proportions; and also, it may be added,
stupidity and insight. He was a typical Briton with
a streak of genius, possibly the only known example.
He could see through a thing, but he could not see
round it. He was visited with sudden flashes of
reality, but he was not gifted with a steady vision.
He had acute perceptions, but no guiding philo-
sophy. He was a respectable man who made fun
of respectability, a sentimentalist who laughed at
sentiment, a patriot who ridiculed patriotism.
Again and again, at the bidding of some powerful
intuition, he exposed a social or national absurdity,
but as often as not he failed to see the point of his
exposure and fell back upon a piece of conventional
claptrap which was equally typical of him. His
sudden exhibitions of daring and insight, coupled
with his native caution and conventionality, made
his work uneven and incalculable, and it was
Sullivan's music that rendered it wholly palatable

to the Victorians. The Englishman is perhaps the only man in the world who can laugh at himself; add music to the satire and he brings the house down, for music removes the sting of reality. Nevertheless, the chief powers in the land never quite got over the "contempt of court" shown in *Trial by Jury*, the contempt of cabinets in *Pinafore*, and the continuous digs at authority in the rest of the operas, culminating with the contempt of the Royal Court in *Utopia*; and they took their only possible revenge. The average Englishman laughed, applauded and whistled the delectable tunes; the important Englishman watched, smiled wryly and sometimes writhed inwardly.

Gilbert's prudence and childlike simplicity were never more conspicuously displayed together than in his statement to Sullivan that, since the First Lord in the opera was a violent radical, while the well-known publisher was a pronounced conservative, there could be no suspicion that W. H. Smith was intended. He was, however, quite right. No one entertained the least suspicion on the point. Everyone was absolutely certain about it. And within a few weeks of the production Disraeli was referring to "*Pinafore* Smith."

Owing to the fact that London was visited by a heat-wave that summer, the audiences at the Opera Comique varied in size and the directors had periodical fits of panic. They announced the withdrawal of the piece about once a fortnight and cancelled the announcement whenever the receipts went up. D'Oyly Carte calmed them to the best of his ability, but both he and the company were kept on tenterhooks for months owing to the nervous condition of his co-directors. Then two things happened to give the show a fillip. Sullivan, who was conducting the Promenade Concerts at Convent Garden, included an arrangement of the *Pinafore* music in one evening's programme. It was liked so much that crowds of concert-goers visited the opera, which was running to good houses by the end of August. Next came the news that *Pinafore* had taken New York by storm and was playing to enormous business at no less than eight theatres; and since England was just beginning to model her taste on that of America, and America was just beginning to accept everything English as a model of taste, *Pinafore* soon became the rage in both countries.

Of course it was pirated in America. There was no copyright agreement between the two countries; and unless the author of a play could produce it on the spot, before anyone else could steal it and produce it first, he could whistle for his royalties. American publishers and theatrical managers made fortunes out of *Pinafore* while Gilbert and Sullivan gnashed their teeth in impotence. Adding insult to injury, the Americans put in a number of local "gags," songs about "pants" (which they have an incurable habit of rhyming with "dance") and such-like unsuitable sallies. Gilbert, Sullivan and Carte decided that something had to be done about it, and the latter sailed for America to take stock of the situation.

During his absence a crisis occurred at the Opera Comique. The lease of the theatre expired at the end of July, 1879, and Carte had determined, now that Gilbert and Sullivan opera seemed a fairly safe investment, to wind up the company and carry on the business himself. The collaborators, weary of the panic-stricken methods of the other members of the board, stood behind Carte, who bought out his co-directors. But the nightly spectacle of packed houses had an inspiriting effect on the retiring directors, who decided to claim the scenery as their property and to put the production on at another theatre. On the last night of their régime they broke into the back of the Opera Comique with a gang of hired roughs and attempted to remove the scenery and properties by force. Their intrusion occurred towards the end of the performance, and the audience, hearing the noise, thought that a fire had broken out. Grossmith walked down to the footlights, explained the situation to the people in front, and after a free fight between chorus and roughs, much enjoyed by the audience, the intruders were kicked out and the performance was concluded. Summonses were promptly issued, and the raiding directors were publicly rebuked in court; but they produced *Pinafore* at the Imperial Theatre and later transferred it to the Olympic, almost next door to the Opera Comique. Gilbert and Sullivan issued a public statement to the effect that the production at the Opera Comique was the authorised version, but playgoers filled both houses for some time in order to make their own comparisons.

In the summer of that year a long report from Carte persuaded Gilbert and Sullivan to visit America in order to give their authorised version of *Pinafore* in New York. Before leaving, Sullivan underwent an operation for crushing the stone in the kidney, and received felicitations upon its success from the Prince of Wales and the Duke of Edinburgh. Gilbert was suffering from a different complaint. "I will not have another libretto of mine produced if the Americans are going to steal it," he declared: "not that I need the money so much, but it upsets my digestion."

4

Reporters swooped down upon them the instant their boat reached New York and the American public, through the medium of its press, was quickly introduced to the two famous visitors: the librettist, a tall military-looking gentleman, with fair hair, rosy complexion, bright blue eyes and high massive forehead, who spoke quickly and jerkily in a deep hearty voice; the composer, a short, plump, daintily-clad person, with a thick neck, dark hair and eyes, olive-tinted mobile face, sensuous lips and tender expression, whose voice was wistful and full of feeling. They were interviewed so thoroughly that Sullivan wondered "Where do all these Americans end?" and Gilbert ceased to wonder. Each of them took pains to make it known that he had done far better work than *Pinafore* unaided by the other. Gilbert said it was a little mortifying to find that a trifle like *Pinafore* should so far exceed in success the plays he held in more serious estimation. Sullivan regretted that his oratorios and other compositions of a more classical and ambitious style had not received the popular approval accorded to *Pinafore*. Neither of them felt unduly flattered when some judge, in an after-dinner speech, hoped they would be brought before him on the charge of being drunk and disorderly, so that he might repay the pleasure *Pinafore* had given him by letting them off. Nor was Gilbert altogether pleased when an American impresario had the bright idea that they might heap up a pile of dollars if only they would prepare an American version of the piece.

"Say now, Mr. Gilbert," said this gentleman, "all you've got to do is to change H.M.S. to U.S.S., pull down the British ensign, hoist the stars and stripes, and anchor your ship off Jersey beach. Then, in place of your First Lord of the Admiralty, introduce our navy boss. All the re-writing you'd want would be some new words to Bill Bobstay's song—just let him remain an American instead of an Englishman. Now ain't that a cute notion, sir?"

"Well, yes," replied Gilbert thoughtfully, "perhaps your suggestion is a good one, but I see some difficulties in carrying it out. In the first place I'm afraid I'm not sufficiently versed in your vernacular to translate my original English words. The best I could do would be something like this:

> He is Ameri-can!
>> Though he himself has said it,
>> 'Tis not much to his credit,
> That he is Ameri-can!
> For he might have been a Dutchman,
> An Irish, Scotch, or such man,
> Or perhaps an Englishman!
>> But in spite of hanky-panky,
>> He remains a true-born Yankee,
> A cute Ameri-can."

The impresario was delighted; he swore it would save the situation and set New York ablaze. After a few moments' reflection Gilbert gravely abandoned the notion, on the ground that such words might impair the friendly relations between the two countries.

While Gilbert and Sullivan were rehearsing their opera and being entertained and interviewed until their heads swam, the barrel-organs of New York were churning out the tunes of *Pinafore*, the music-shops were flooded with its scores, most of the theatres were playing it, and such was the demand for it throughout the States that one paper announced: "At present there are forty-two companies playing *Pinafore* about the country. Companies formed after six p.m. yesterday are not included." The authorised edition of the work appeared on December 1st at the Fifth Avenue Theatre and received an ovation. Everyone in the audience was of course already familiar with the airs, but the orchestration, with which the numerous American bands had not troubled their heads, was a revelation. It was greeted as a comparatively new work and it looked as if a ninth company were about to coin money in the city. Gilbert, in his speech before the curtain after the first performance, said: "It has been our purpose to produce something that should be innocent but not imbecile." That was the slogan of the collaborators: clean but clever fun. They had made up their minds, they said, to do all in their power to wipe out the grosser elements of early Victorian burlesque, "Never to let an evil word escape our characters, and never to allow a

man to appear as a woman or vice versa." That
Gilbert's intention was entirely successful is vouched
for by Dean Welldon: "He wrote no play, nor even
perhaps a line, that the sensitive modesty of a
young girl might shrink from hearing."

Lewis Carroll would not have endorsed the
Dean's verdict, though it is possible that the
author of *Alice in Wonderland* had a personal motive
for his distress. Carroll had written to Sullivan in
March, 1877, begging him to set some of the songs
in *Alice* to music. Sullivan had replied that he was
extremely busy and would require too much money.
Carroll had pressed him to name his terms, but
Sullivan had obtained a copy of *Alice*, had studied
it carefully and had decided that he could do nothing with the odd metre of the songs. Eleven years
later Carroll witnessed a performance of *Pinafore* by
children and was so much shocked by it that he
felt impelled to write his impressions for the
Theatre. He started off with *The Sorcerer*, describing
a song, *The Pale Young Curate*, as "simply painful."
Having pictured the distressing life of a pale young
curate in the slums, he asked his readers whether
they could "*laugh* at that man." If they could, then
they must also laugh "at that pale young soldier, as
he sinks on the trampled battlefield, and reddens
the dust with his life-blood for the honour of Old
England!" The Pale Young Curate was bad
enough, but what could be said of *H.M.S. Pinafore*

with a cast of children? He found one passage "sad beyond words. It occurs when the captain utters the oath 'Damn me!' and forthwith a bevy of sweet, innocent-looking girls sing, with bright and happy looks, the chorus 'He said, Damn me! He said, Damn me!' I cannot find words to convey to the reader the pain I felt in seeing these dear children taught to utter such words to amuse ears grown callous to their ghastly meaning. Put the two ideas side by side—Hell (no matter whether *you* believe in it or not; millions do) and those pure young lips thus sporting with its horrors—and then find what *fun* in it you can! How Mr. Gilbert could have stooped to write, or Sir Arthur Sullivan could have prostituted his noble art to set to music, such vile trash, it passes my skill to understand." From which it appears that, with some Victorians, fun had to be not only clean but grim.

But the Carroll view was not taken in America, and if the piece had not already been whistled and quoted until it became a point of honour in decent society not to do either, the new and true version might have run for years. As things were, business appreciably slackened after the first outburst of excitement, and Sullivan began to work feverishly on the new opera which Gilbert had completed before leaving England. This was *The Pirates of Penzance*. Sullivan had written the songs for the second act when he received the libretto and had sketched out a number of songs in the first act. The second act he had brought with him, but he had carelessly left the sketches for the first act at home, and now had to re-write from memory. Between public dinners, visitors, attacks of pain, rehearsals of the completed second act, and his job as conductor at the theatre, he managed somehow to finish the first act and score the entire work during December, though he seldom got to bed until 5.30 in the morning. Just before the opening night he had trouble with the band, the members of which voted that *The Pirates* came under the heading of Grand Opera, which entitled them to higher rates of pay. The position was not improved by the manager of the theatre, who told them that they should be content with the high honour of being conducted by England's greatest composer, for it occurred to them that they should be paid more for the high honour as well as for the Grand Opera, and they raised both points when threatening to down instruments. Sullivan adroitly turned the tables on them. He disclaimed the greatness that had been thrust upon him and said that he felt the honour of conducting such a brilliant orchestra. He even hinted that his work was not worthy of them and that, if they felt so too, he should wire at once to England for a less sensitive orchestra. They agreed to abase themselves on the same terms as before.

On the night of December 30th, after the final dress-rehearsal, Sullivan returned to his hotel and began work on the overture, finishing it at five o'clock on the morning of the 31st, and rehearsing it six hours later. He was not well enough to eat that day, so went to bed in the afternoon and tried to sleep. Still feeling wretchedly ill and worn out with fatigue, for he could not sleep, he rose, dressed slowly, and wandered off to a club, where he had twelve oysters and a glass of champagne. More dead than alive, he went on to the theatre, took his place in the orchestra, lifted his baton, and *The Pirates of Penzance* swept New York off its feet.

Beyond drawing on his forgotten opera, *Thespis*, for a chorus, Gilbert had taken great pains with this new work, and the result was so delightfully fresh that no one took exception even to the Pirate King's remark: "I don't think much of our profession, but, contrasted with respectability, it is comparatively honest." After all, Pirate Kings were allowed to have their bit of fun. But when the piece was produced in London the skit on "the very model of a modern Major-General" was not welcomed in certain quarters:

"For my military knowledge, though I'm plucky
    and adventury,
Has only been brought down to the beginning of
    the century."

Another joke caused grave displeasure in high

places and Gilbert was made to pay for it later on. When the Police say to the Pirates:

> "We charge you yield, in Queen Victoria's
> name,"

the Pirate King replies:

> "We yield at once, with humbled mien,
>> Because, with all our faults, we love our
>> Queen."

There was not much harm in that, though the Queen might not have valued the loyalty of pirates. But when, immediately afterwards, the pirates are excused on the ground that

> "They are no members of the common
> throng;
>> They are all noblemen who have gone
>> wrong!"

and the General exclaims:

> "No Englishman unmoved that statement
> hears,
>> Because, with all our faults, we love our House
>> of Peers,"

several eminent people considered that the hit went past the woolsack to the throne.

However, American sensibilities were not wounded because they were not being attacked, and the Fifth Avenue Theatre did record business. The chief difficulty of the trio, Gilbert-Sullivan-Carte, was to prevent the pirating of *The Pirates*. In America half a century ago a work became anyone's property the moment it was printed; so after every performance the music had to be hidden away in a safe. Large bribes were offered to members of the orchestra to loan their scores, and a careful eye had to be kept on their movements. Musicians were placed in the audience by piratical managers with instructions to jot down the themes, and eventually various fragmentary versions appeared elsewhere; but this time New York had the original work, produced and conducted by the creators themselves, and would not be fobbed off with cheap substitutes. Also the trio decided at once to send out a number of companies on tour, and they worked day and night to forestall those who would cheat them of their rights, rehearsing three or four companies at the same time, and, when they should have been resting, attending numberless social functions. The strain told particularly on Sullivan, still a victim to his old trouble, and sometimes he was found in a semi-conscious condition from pain and overwork. The circumstances which forced the strain upon him rankled in his mind and he was heard to say: "A free and independent American citizen ought not to be robbed of his right of robbing someone else." Gilbert, though equally annoyed, had a stronger constitution, and treated his American acquaintances in a less direct fashion:

"Oh, Mr. Gilbert," said a wealthy lady at some

dinner party, "your friend Mr. Sullivan's music is really too delightful. It reminds me so much of dear Baytch (Bach). Do tell me: what is Baytch doing just now? Is he still composing?"

"Well, no, madam," Gilbert returned, "just now, as a matter of fact, dear Baytch is by way of decomposing."

Having launched their last company at Buffalo, they went to see Niagara Falls. They had made up their minds to return to England in time to produce *The Pirates* for the opening of the spring season. Their boat was to sail on March 3rd, and when they reached Niagara they had ten days to spare. Gilbert went back to New York to settle their affairs. Sullivan went on to Ottawa, where he stayed with Princess Louise and the Marquess of Lorne at Government House; which must have irritated a certain watchmaker's wife, who, unaware of his friendships in royal circles, had refused to dine at some function in New York because Mr. Arthur Sullivan, a mere musician, whose tunes were played on the barrel-organs, had been asked to sit at the same table.

5

Though their biographers have ignored the early signs of discord between the partners, it is at this point that we must note the beginning of a quarrel, the root cause of which lay in their divergent temperaments.   Gilbert, it must always be remembered, was the dominant partner, and Sullivan's admiration of him had something feminine in it.   Gilbert was in a very real sense the begetter of Sullivan's best music; he was the Svengali who by hypnotising Trilby-Sullivan could create the notes he wanted; and Sullivan surrendered gladly to the magnetism of a personality that could extract from him the essence of a lighthearted happiness he was otherwise unable to express.

But there was another side to this artistically ideal partnership.   Gilbert was jealous of the music he had inspired in Sullivan, and Sullivan was annoyed that he should be dependent upon Gilbert. These emotions became stronger as time went on; but in the earlier stages they took the form of banter with Gilbert, of reserve with Sullivan. Wherever Gilbert went he heard people whistling Sullivan's tunes and singing Sullivan's praise. He had no ear for music and little admiration for it, and the constant repetition of melodies that would never have been written but for his words aroused his resentment.   He relieved himself by chaffing Sullivan in public; and though Sullivan had borne it patiently enough in London, the persistent facetiousness of the elder man at his expense whenever they were the guests of honour at social functions in New York jarred upon him and embittered him. When he returned home he complained to Fred Clay that he did not think he could put up with it much longer.

The great success of *The Pirates of Penzance*, which opened at the Opera Comique on April 3rd, 1880, temporarily saved the situation, because in London the partners never met outside business, and there was no business to bring them together until a successor to the new opera should be required. Acting probably on the advice of Fred Clay, Sullivan made a gesture of friendship to Gilbert after *The Pirates* was produced. It may have been his way of hinting that Gilbert should in future supply him with more serious libretti, for he always entertained the curious belief that solemn music was more important than light music, but whatever his reason he asked Gilbert to prepare a verse-version of *The Martyr of Antioch*, which he was writing for the Leeds Festival.

Gilbert, who liked being mistaken for a poet, at once complied. The work was produced in the autumn and dedicated to the Princess of Wales. Grave musicians again acclaimed Sullivan as a master and wondered how a man who was capable of writing such a moving anthem in his latest oratorio as "Brother, Thou Hast Gone Before Us" could go on setting music to such nonsense as "When the enterprising burglar's not a-burgling," which was being received with roars of applause at the Opera Comique. Such was its success, indeed, that Rutland Barrington, as the Sergeant of Police, had to repeat the last verse at least twice every night. It therefore occurred to him that an "encore" verse would add emormously to the popularity of the song, and he asked Gilbert to write him one.

" 'Encore' means 'sing it again,' " was Gilbert's curt response.

But *The Pirates* could not last for ever, and Gilbert was already hard at work on a successor. The æsthetic craze was then at its height. Oscar Wilde was to be seen in Piccadilly in fancy-dress; and the philistines, led by George Du Maurier in *Punch*, were indulging in the popular pastime of pelting poets. Gilbert, who had a good eye to business, saw which way the wind was blowing and determined to add a few puffs of his own. Then he had a fit of laziness. Why not base his libretto on *The Rival Curates*, one of the *Bab Ballads*? Curates were more absurd than æsthetes, who had been sufficiently castigated by Du Maurier and Burnand. Besides, he really disliked the affectations of parsons and he hated the way in which they were idolised by women. His objection to the clergy was notorious. Staying in some provincial hotel, he once found himself the only layman among a number of divines who were present for a conference in the town, one of whom addressed him with quiet irony:

"I should think, Mr. Gilbert, you must feel slightly out of place in this company?"

"Yes," answered Gilbert, "I feel like a lion in a den of Daniels."

So, between laziness and inclination, he began a libretto which should hold the typical curate up to ridicule. He had not been working on it for long when he was attacked by severe twinges of caution. Would it be popular? Would people be amused by a chorus of comical curates? Would it not be thought that he was laughing at religion? Even with the music of a devout composer of oratorios . . . no, it was too dangerous. Instantly he switched round, reverted to the original plan, and with a sigh of relief went after safer game.

Sullivan, the success of whose recent oratorio had made him dissatisfied with lesser themes, packed a part of *Patience* in his bag, dismissed the subject from his mind, and departed for a holiday of two months in the Riviera and Italy, where he interested himself in a scheme to float a tramway company. He was back in London by the middle of February, 1881, and helped Gilbert and Carte with the lawsuit they were bringing against the Comedy Opera Company to prevent the latter from performing their works. After the case was won, he settled down to *Patience*, though, as was usual with him, he had to work overtime to get it finished by the day of production. He started to score the work ten days before the first night, and began to sketch out the overture forty-eight hours before the curtain went up.

Patience was first seen at the Opera Comique on April 23rd, 1881, and had an immense success. The theatre in Wych Street could not hold the people who rushed to see it, and D'Oyly Carte, who had for some time been building a permanent home for Gilbert and Sullivan Opera, was able to transfer it on October 10th to the Savoy Theatre, which was the first playhouse in London to be lighted with electricity, and where the queue system for unreserved seats was first instituted. The opening night at the new theatre was the occasion for a great social display; the Prince of Wales was there, Sullivan conducted (as he always did when the Prince came), and after the performance he took the Prince behind the scenes and presented the principal members of the company to him.

Incidentally, Sullivan had just been doing a round of royalties, rather to Gilbert's disgust. The Duke of Edinburgh, who was in command of the Reserve Squadron, had invited him for a cruise on H.M.S. *Hercules* to St. Petersburg, and during the summer of '81 he accompanied the squadron, making the acquaintance of sundry Baltic monarchs and princes, one of whom, afterwards Kaiser Wilhelm II, paid him the compliment

of singing "He polished up the handle of the big
front door," somewhat to Sullivan's discomfort.
They ran into a thick fog on the way back, and the
Duke spent thirty hours on the bridge of the
Hercules explaining that he was responsible for the
safety of "eight ironclads, some thousands of lives
and a musical composer." Meanwhile Gilbert was
risking the life of an operatic librettist in a little
yacht, which slipped in and out of harbours on the
south coast of England, unattended by flags,
bands and royal salutes. Each of them, in his own
way, enjoyed his holiday.

Patience was clearly in for a long run, and though
Gilbert talked vaguely of their next piece, which he
called *Iolanthe*, Sullivan scarcely gave it a moment's
thought. Instead he took advantage of the pre-
vailing prosperity and moved into his final home,
No. 1 Queen's Mansions, a forbidding block of
flats in Queen Victoria Street. After that he set
out for Egypt, where he spent three lazy months,
sending glowing accounts to his mother from Cairo
of dervish dancers, Arabian music, official dinners,
Moslem processions, visits to the Khedive, and an
evening of riotous games with the Duke of Clarence
and Prince George (King George V) who "knocked
me about a good deal."

He was back in London for his fortieth birthday
in May, 1882, and then the third and most poignant
tragedy of his life cast a shadow over his days that

was never entirely dispelled. His mother died. She was the last and best-loved of the little circle in which he had grown up and within which alone he could find sanctuary. He experienced a sense of loneliness so dreadful that he tried to escape it in the throes of composition, beginning the music of *Iolanthe*, working hard through each night and destroying nearly all he had done when next he sat down to try again. He now had his brother's widow and children entirely on his hands, and one of them, Herbert Sullivan, he adopted.

By this time he had formed another connection of vital importance in his life. Mrs. Ronalds was one of the famous beauties of the day. She was a wealthy American, whose marriage had not been a success, and she lived apart from her husband. She had an exceptionally fine voice, was a great friend of the Empress Eugénie, and after the fall of the Third Empire had come to London and taken a house at No. 7 Cadogan Place, where her *salons* were attended by royalty and the pick of London society. The Prince of Wales declared that he would travel the length of England to hear her sing *The Lost Chord*, her rendering of which moved the composer to tears. A deep and abiding friendship was formed between Sullivan and Mrs. Ronalds; they met daily, and when they were separated by distance they wrote or telegraphed to one another every day. After his mother's death their friendship became closer than ever and her influence over him more complete. It was generally believed that she was his mistress, and though his official biographers have implied that their relationship was platonic, it is difficult not to echo the comment of an American biographer: "Is it likely?" Everything, in fact, points to an intimacy of a more normal nature. Sullivan allowed her to attend auditions at the Savoy Theatre, which did not help to put the more nervous singers at their ease, and followed her advice on most matters with a whole-heartedness seldom displayed by husbands when proffered counsel by their wives.

The summer of 1882 found Sullivan in Cornwall, where he was staying with friends, writing the music for *Iolanthe* and playing poker. He did not care for the first act of the new opera, and asked Gilbert to meet him and talk it over. Gilbert was yachting on the south coast, and the meeting took place in the coffee-room of the Half Moon Hotel in Exeter, where they started the afternoon with ham and eggs and ended it with a new act. Since *Patience* had been pirated all over America, they decided to send over a company of *Iolanthe* and produce it simultaneously in New York and London. As usual, Sullivan was late with the music; fits of laziness were followed by spurts of overwork, which brought on a severe attack of his kidney complaint; but by labouring steadily through the nights, sometimes until six or seven in the morning, he contrived to finish the job four days before the opening performance.

On November 25th, 1882, the curtain of the Savoy Theatre went up on an Arcadian landscape and came down to thunderous applause. Gilbert and Sullivan had scored another enormous success. It meant more to Sullivan than to his collaborator, because, just before leaving home that night, he had heard of the bankruptcy of the stockbrokers with whom all his securities were deposited, and the consequent loss of the whole of his life's savings.

6

Gilbert's securities were more secure. By 1883 he was busy building himself a house at No. 39 Harrington Gardens, South Kensington, and here he lived until 1890; though he also had a house called "Breakspears" at Uxbridge for the summer months, playing a lot of tennis there and extending the length of the court because he found it difficult to keep a ball within the regulation limits. Having more money than he needed for a livelihood, he lavished it on his new London home. His family arms and crest appeared over the doorway, carved on a shield of stone and supported by birds held by cupids. An Elizabethan navigator named Sir Humphrey Gilbert, who founded the first English

E

colony in North America, was claimed as an ancestor, and Gilbert commemorated him by placing a stone ship on the gable of the house. When someone asked whether the ship was *H.M.S. Pinafore* he answered hotly: "I do not put my trademark on the top of my house."   Ornate chimneypieces, panelled walls, oak beams, heavily-moulded ceilings, stained-glass windows, elaborate wall-papers and tapestries were in evidence throughout the house, which was fitted up with all the latest improvements—really novel in 1883—telephone, electric light, central heating, a bathroom on every floor, and so forth.   In this remarkable mansion, which still retains many of its original characteristics, Gilbert wrote three of his most famous operas (*The Mikado*, *The Yeomen of the Guard* and *The Gondoliers*) and two less-famous ones (*Princess Ida* and *Ruddigore*) seated comfortably in an armchair in his study.   This house, and no other, is therefore the Mecca of all true Gilbertians.

Gilbert hated waste, and the plot of *Iolanthe*, like so many songs and ideas in the other operas, was taken from a *Bab Ballad*.   His gibes at peers and M.P.s throughout this opera were soon the talk of every club, and both lords and commoners had to pretend they were enjoying the joke as much as anyone; but it was lucky for Gilbert that he was too successful to be attacked or ignored.   His next libretto was founded on a play he had written fourteen years earlier, *The Princess*, which was itself a parody of Tennyson's poem. To save himself trouble he lifted chunks of dialogue from the earlier work and transferred it bodily to *Princess Ida*, which thus became a blank-verse opera. It was produced on January 5th, 1884, and compared with its predecessors it might have been described as a failure, for it only reached a total of 246 performances. .

Sullivan at first did not like it, and "a slight breeze" occurred between the two, but after Gilbert had dealt with his objections he was pacified. In May, 1883, before he began to write the music, Sullivan was knighted, and *The Musical Review* came out with the statement that it would henceforth be *infra dig* for *Sir* Arthur Sullivan to write music to *Mr*. W. S. Gilbert's words, a sentiment that found constant expression, from now on, in the graver periodicals of the day and in the mouths of those friends who believed that Sullivan was frittering away his gifts and who failed to see that the original and highly individual work he was doing with Gilbert was incomparably better than the echoes of Mendelssohn, Auber and Gounod which were heard too often in his oratorios and incidental music. It may be noted as a curious feature of the Victorian Age that "grave" work was, for the first time in English art, exalted above "gay" work. Gilbert himself accepted this convention and rated his solemn plays far more highly than his amusing operas. The Elizabethans had a more balanced and realistic view of life, and it would never have occurred to them, or to any age before the Victorian, that tragedy was superior to comedy or that Hamlet was a higher manifestation of genius than Falstaff.

Sullivan listened to these earnest promptings with one ear, and their effect upon him will shortly be apparent, but he had another ear for the siren voices that sang of social advancement and financial success. He knew to whom he was chiefly indebted for his knighthood, and on his forty-first birthday he gave a dinner-party to the Prince of Wales, the Duke of Edinburgh, several peers of the realm and a commoner or two, including Gilbert. A musical entertainment followed, in which some of the leading singers of the day took part, and at a quarter past eleven Sullivan surprised his royal guests by ringing up the Savoy Theatre on the telephone. It was a Sunday night and he had asked the company playing *Iolanthe* to do selections from the opera at the theatre, so that his guests might enjoy the novelty of "listening-in" by means of an electrophone which he had had installed at his flat. The Prince was delighted; everyone was delighted; except perhaps Gilbert, who did not care for princes or prima-donnas, and believed that the opera, especially the words, could have been enjoyed with more advantage to all concerned from a box or stall at the Savoy Theatre the following evening.

It may have been Sullivan's knighthood or it may have been Sullivan's criticism that ruffled Gilbert and caused a certain amount of friction during the rehearsals of *Princess Ida*. The actors did not take kindly to the blank verse, and Gilbert was frequently forced to correct them. One gentleman, exasperated by repeated promptings, burst out:

"Look here, sir, I will *not* be bullied. I know my lines."

"That may be so, but you don't know mine," snapped Gilbert.

Grossmith had several brushes with the producer, and after one of the latter's sharp comments said indignantly:

"I beg your pardon!"

"I accept the apology," retorted Gilbert; "let's get on with the rehearsal."

At last Grossmith could endure it no longer. He had been made to go over the same scene twenty times in succession and when told to do so again he exploded:

"I've rehearsed this confounded business until I feel a perfect fool!"

"Ah," said Gilbert, "now we can talk on equal terms."

Sullivan had his troubles too. His friend, Fred Clay, had a paralytic stroke in December, 1883, followed by another within twenty-four hours, and Sullivan was so upset that he could not work, though the date of production was but three weeks ahead. Then, to make up for lost time, he worked day and night together. Since he was constantly putting off his work he was constantly overworked, and the strain of overwork always brought a return of his malady. As with *Iolanthe*, he finished the music four days before the date of production, and then the reaction set in. Brain and body collapsed. On the afternoon of January 5th the doctor, convinced that his patient would be unable to conduct the performance, injected morphia to ease his pain. At seven o'clock Sullivan took another injection and a cup of black coffee. Slowly and painfully he dragged himself out of bed, was helped into his clothes by his valet, and drove to the Savoy. Half-conscious he entered the orchestra. A terrific reception braced him and he got through the evening without difficulty. But after his "call" with Gilbert before the curtain he fainted and was taken home by friends.

Though the first performance of *Princess Ida* was rapturously received, the blank verse was not in the Gilbert and Sullivan tradition, and playgoers were disappointed. The actors, too, did not care for their parts, and Rutland Barrington attributed the comparative failure of the piece to the fact that King Hildebrand was not given sufficient prominence. He was playing the part himself, which may conceivably have influenced his opinion.

CHAPTER IV

GILBERT AND SULLIVAN

I

THE strain he had undergone during the production of the last opera, the references in the press to the weighty duties of a composer who had been honoured by his Sovereign, the solemn admonitions of George Grove and George Macfarren, both of whom had been knighted with him, and the fact that he felt ill and played-out, forced Sullivan to a decision. He informed D'Oyly Carte that, tired of light opera, he did not intend to write anything more for the Savoy Theatre. Carte was thunderstruck. At first he did not believe that Sullivan was serious, but after dining with the composer he changed his mind: Sullivan was deadly serious. But Carte was a business man, and having failed to coax Sullivan, he threatened him. The trio had recently signed an agreement for five years, whereby Gilbert and Sullivan had bound themselves to provide operas for the Savoy during that period, Carte to give them six months' notice whenever a new work should be required. By the end of

March it was clear that *Princess Ida* would not repeat the success of its forerunners, and Carte despatched a formal notification to the collaborators, at the same time informing Gilbert of Sullivan's attitude.

Gilbert was amazed and promptly wrote to Sullivan for an explanation. Sullivan replied from the British Legation in Brussels, and it is clear from his letter that Carte's reminder of the agreement, which rendered the collaborators liable for any losses resulting from their failure to supply an opera, had made him shift his ground. He said that his music was becoming repetitive and that his work had been dominated by Gilbert's words. He wanted greater freedom; he wanted his music to "speak for itself"; he wanted "a story of human interest and probability"; he implied that Gilbert had a habit of spoiling a serious scene by the introduction of humorous dialogue; above all he wanted a libretto in which the humorous and serious elements were kept entirely separate. This letter gave Gilbert "considerable pain," and in his answer he assumed that it had been written in a hurry, since he could not suppose that Sullivan had meant to "gall and wound" him. He accused Sullivan of trying to teach him the A B C of his profession, and left it at that.

A fortnight later they met at Sullivan's flat and talked for two hours. Gilbert had what he considered an excellent subject for their next work, but unfortunately he had been similarly inspired about two years before and Sullivan had turned it down as artificial. The main idea was that by swallowing a lozenge a person became the character he or she pretended to be. Gilbert was obsessed by this theme; it cropped up at nearly every stage of his future dealings with Sullivan; and eventually he collaborated with Alfred Cellier and used it in *The Mountebanks*. By then he had changed the lozenge to a liquid, and this is what we read: "Man is a hypocrite and invariably affects to be better and wiser than he really is. This liquid, which should be freely diluted, has the effect of making everyone who drinks it exactly what he pretends to be. The hypocrite becomes a man of piety; the swindler a man of honour; the quack a man of learning; and the braggart a man of war." Not perhaps a particularly brilliant notion, but it captured the imagination of Gilbert, and Sullivan had to pay for it. Their two hours' talk about the effect of the lozenge came to nothing. Sullivan could not stomach the unreality of the plot—and in fairness to him one has to admit that probability is not its strong point—while Gilbert was really suffering from lozenge on the brain.

The next move came from Gilbert, who wrote suggesting that if Carte agreed Sullivan should do his next opera with someone else. Gilbert went

E*

on to say that he was at a loss to know what Sullivan wanted from him and that Sullivan's objections to his libretto seemed to him "arbitrary and capricious"; yet another proof of the strange lack of sympathy and understanding between the men, a variation in humanity that somehow produced a fusion in art. Sullivan refused to entertain the suggestion and hinted that Gilbert might evolve another plot. But Gilbert remained faithful to his lozenge, and in order to meet Sullivan's demand for "human interest," promised to separate the serious and comic episodes, keeping each firmly in its place. Sullivan, though still protesting against the lozenge, was partly pacified and agreed to give his "most earnest consideration" to the plot when Gilbert had fully sketched it out. Gilbert finished the job in a few days and went to read the result to Sullivan, who liked it much better than before, but again displayed hostility to the lozenge. However, he promised to study it carefully and let Gilbert have his final opinion shortly. He wrestled with the theme in solitude for several days, but the lozenge stuck in his throat, and at length he had to confess that the plot did not arouse in him that "enthusiasm which has hitherto characterized all my work with you" and without which he would not undergo the pangs of composition. He advised Gilbert to write a piece which should be innocent of supernatural or improbable elements.

Gilbert lost his temper. Had not Sullivan expressly declared his satisfaction with the plot only a few days before? Gilbert had made his reputation and his fortune on the exploitation of the supernatural and the improbable and he was certainly not going to be told at this time of the day that he must forgo his fairies or his lozenges. Taking up his pen, he wrote: "The time has arrived when I must state . . . that I cannot consent to construct another plot for the next opera." He wrote reluctantly, he said, and remained "Yours truly." Sullivan replied that further discussion would obviously be useless, that he regretted it very much, and remained "Yours sincerely."

Carte nearly went off his head when he heard what had happened. Had he known how much money their next opera was destined to make, the anxiety caused by the present uncertainty might have killed him. He rushed from Gilbert to Sullivan and from Sullivan to Gilbert in a fever of friendliness, and at last, after each had stood upon his dignity for a period sufficient to satisfy his pride, the business argument prevailed. Gilbert agreed to jettison the lozenge and all it stood for, and Sullivan was so relieved that he undertook to set the new piece without even asking what the subject was to be.

The quarrel had cleared the air, and in an atmosphere of good-will and serenity the partners produced a work that was the perfect expression of their artistic harmony.

Gilbert had a clearer conception of what the public wanted than Sullivan; he led and Sullivan followed. "I know my limitations and capabilities better than anyone else," he once said; "no man is successful until he learns that lesson"; which was certainly true when he was writing libretti. But he also knew that success was not solely the result of self-knowledge. "The secret of success," he said, "is to keep well within the understanding of the least intelligent section of the audience." This did not call for a very high order of merit on the part of the author, he admitted, though it required a good deal of practical skill. He worked with the utmost care, often between eleven at night and three or four in the morning, because "then you have absolute peace—the postman has done his worst and no one can interrupt you unless it be a burglar."

He usually began by writing out the story of the piece about twelve times, until he had got it right. He then read it to Sullivan, who sometimes made suggestions, which were duly incorporated in the final version. After that he commenced the libretto, writing only the baldest dialogue and leaving out both songs and jokes. This merely carried on the action in the fewest possible words. Later he wrote the songs for the first act, which were sent to Sullivan, who set them to music while Gilbert was writing the songs for the second act. The songs completed, Gilbert returned to the dialogue, elaborated and polished the crude suggestions in the first draft and filled it out with the necessary number of jokes. The reason he would not allow the actors to "gag" was because he had so carefully timed the "laughs" that an additional joke, perhaps in the wrong place, might have destroyed the dramatic or humorous value of the scene as he visualised it. Very occasionally he permitted an actor to put in a quip or a piece of business that did not happen to spoil the effect of what followed, but his usual reaction to that kind of thing was neatly expressed when Grossmith, anxious to score a "laugh" during one of his scenes, fell over and rolled on the floor.

"Kindly omit that," said Gilbert sternly.

"Certainly, if you wish it," replied Grossmith, "but I get an enormous laugh by it."

"So you would if you sat on a pork-pie," was Gilbert's comment.

On the other hand, he was quite willing to receive suggestions from actors as to how their parts should be played. At a revival of *Pinafore* Walter Passmore asked him:

"Don't you think that I ought to play Sir Joseph with his nose in the air, as if he was raising it above an unpleasant smell?"

"Unpleasant smell," muttered Gilbert, lifting an

eyebrow; "well, you're the best judge of that, Passmore."

Gilbert's vitality as a producer was phenomenal. He supervised everything—scenery, costumes, stage-management, chorus, lighting—and nothing escaped his notice. His attention to detail was such that Barrington once betted he would not commence a rehearsal of *Pinafore* before noticing that one of the ship's ropes was wrongly placed, and won the bet. His strictness at rehearsals has become proverbial, and he certainly could play the martinet, but no producer since his time has been able to exercise half his patience. He would stand on the stage by the side of an actor or actress and repeat the words with appropriate action over and over again, without the least sign of despair or irritation, until he had achieved the exact intonation and gesture he wanted. He knew the limitations of his actors and took care that the work he gave them to do should be well within their compass. He also knew that he could only get the best out of them by being on friendly terms with them. He believed that acting could not only be taught but dictated, and it satisfied his appetite for power to teach his actors like children who did not know their alphabet. With those who took his teaching in good part and tried their hardest to follow it, his patience was inexhaustible and his kindliness never-failing. To one well-meaning girl who kept putting the accent on the wrong syllable of the word "in-dubitably," he remarked that hers was a Parisian pronunciation and though of course it would be understood by the stalls it might not be clear to the gallery. He had a different method of dealing with those who resented his teaching and refused to follow it. To a girl who was evidently not trying to obey his instructions, he said: "Never mind, my dear, you cannot help it; it takes a lady to get it as I want it." Naturally his moods varied. Sometimes he was all smiles, and the actors breathed freely. At other times he glowered upon the assembled company, and no one dared to approach him. Whenever he was exceptionally irritable the actors would assume that he had been eating almond rock, of which he was very fond; and as it was supposed to be bad for his gout an "Almond Rock Day" was usually tempestuous.

He was to be seen at his best and at his worst when drilling the chorus. Then the military-looking gentleman became military in manner. He issued his words of command as if he were on parade, and when they were not obeyed he stormed and shouted. Sometimes he would even seize the leader of the chorus and shake him into a Gilbertian view of his duties. He seemed to be possessed of demons. When the dancers failed to put sufficient vigour into their performance he would show them how to do it by twirling up and down the stage, his coat-tails flying, his square sporting hat jammed hard on his head, his feet moving at a most un-military speed and his body gyrating in a manner never seen on the drill-ground. Even though he could not sing a note in tune, he would instruct the chorus in rhythm and pronunciation. However rapidly uttered, every word had to be given its full value, every syllable its proper inflection.

"Remember, ladies and gentlemen," he would bawl, "you've got—to—do—your—damnedest in this passage, or it'll go flat!"

At the close of one of these drastic rehearsals the female chorus were speechless, the male chorus were spineless, and all of them were thirsty. But they had a very high opinion of him, and one of them reverently paid him this tribute: "He's the only man I ever met who could swear straight on for five minutes without stopping to think and without repeating himself."

He was not always so vigorous. Some playful moods have been recorded. During the rehearsals of a certain opera the male chorus had to raise their right hands at a given moment, but every time they did so one of their number raised his left hand by mistake. At last Gilbert said: "My good fellow, if you don't know your right, ask the gentle-man on your left." Once he was directing a dress-rehearsal of *The Mikado* from the centre of the stalls and suddenly called out:

"There's a gentleman in the left group not holding his fan correctly."

The stage-manager at once came forward to say that the offender was a temporary substitute: "One gentleman is absent through illness, sir," he explained.

"Ah, that is not the gentleman I am referring to," replied Gilbert.

Sometimes he had to ease an awkward situation created by a member of the chorus. A girl who had just joined the company complained that one of the gentlemen choristers had put his arm round her waist and called her "a pretty dear." Gilbert mollified her at once with: "Never mind, never mind; he couldn't have meant it."

He did not usually treat such matters with levity, and the moral atmosphere behind the scenes at the Savoy Theatre would have been approved by Queen Victoria herself. The strictest discipline was enforced by Gilbert and no theatre was ever run with such careful regard to propriety. The dressing-rooms of the actors were on one side of the stage, those of the actresses on the other; no lingering about the corridors or on the stage was allowed, no gossiping of the sexes in one another's dressing rooms; when not actually playing or waiting for their entrances on the scene, the performers had no contact with one another in the theatre. Even on the stage they were not safe from the eye of authority, and every time they varied from the set "business" of the piece or mis-quoted the text they were fined half-a-crown.

This monastic or conventual austerity was also observed at rehearsals, and though Gilbert was heard to swear he was never heard to use an ambiguous word. His language, like his libretti, was clean, if hearty. An innuendo from a member of the company would have produced an explosion, and probably an expulsion, and it was a black-letter day in the annals of the Savoy when Gilbert, explaining to the chorus how the word "politely" should be accented in a song, said: "The ladies *must* go down on the 'po.' " The tittering that followed his order was sternly checked. One well-known singer left the company after a few rehearsals, and Gilbert gave a curt explanation of her abrupt departure: "My companies consist of ladies and gentlemen, and she was impossible."

According to Jessie Bond, he "watched over us young women like a dragon." During the run of *Patience* he happened one evening to be standing by the side of Jessie when a note was brought to her.

"What's that, Jessie—a love-letter?" he asked.

"Here it is; you can look for yourself," she answered, handing him the note, which was from a party of four young men in one of the stage-boxes asking her to have supper with them after the performance.

Gilbert was extremely angry; he considered that the letter was an insult to a lady and instantly went round to acquaint the young men with his views. The young men were ignorant of the standard of behaviour enforced at the Savoy Theatre, and the sudden appearance in their box of what they took to be an irate colonel (probably Indian Army, retired, with a troublesome liver) completely upset their conceptions of life behind the scenes. Unable to give any satisfactory reasons for their past existence at a moment's notice, their immediate future was placed on an optional basis by their liverish visitor, who said:

"There are three ways of dealing with you, and you can take your choice. I will go before the curtain, if you like, explain what has happened, and say that Miss Bond refuses to continue whilst you are here, or you can go of your own accord, or I can send a couple of commissionaires to carry you."

They chose the second, and probably entertained morbid views of light opera for the rest of their lives. The incident got into the comic papers, the "Savoy Boarding School" became the joke of the season, and Jessie Bond received printed condolences, e.g., "Poor little dear! she always has to show her love-letters to her daddy!"

Though Gilbert carried his views on respectability to a point that some thought was beyond the limit,

his attitude was not entirely unreasonable.   In
those days actresses were popularly supposed to be
saleable property. Their social status was extremely
low, and the average middle-class Englishman
scarcely differentiated the back of the stage from a
brothel.   A Victorian Dr. Johnson (if one can
imagine such a being) would have defined an
actress in his dictionary as an immoral woman.
Jessie Bond's husband, for example, came of a
Quaker family, and when after their wedding
Jessie got into the carriage to drive away, her
father-in-law's parting words were: "I hope you
are going to be faithful to Lewis, Jessie."   When
Gilbert was not on the premises even the actresses
at the Savoy were made to feel that they were not
"ladies."   One evening Jessie and several others
were sitting in the green-room when the door
opened and in walked Carte, followed by the
Prince of Wales and a few friends.   The ladies
stood up, but no one took the least notice of them,
and the Prince, having made himself comfortable
in a chair, proceeded to light a cigar. Jessie Bond
promptly sat down and went on with her sewing,
much to the annoyance of Carte, who made angry
signs, unperceived by the Prince, that she should
remain standing. Later she was scolded for her
behaviour by Carte, but she replied that he ought
to have presented them to the Prince. Later still
she met the Prince at Sullivan's flat, reminded him

of the incident and informed him that "there *are* ladies in our profession."

"Miss Bond," said he, "you are perfectly right."

To prove the sincerity of his conversion to her view, he made a request:

"May I come to see you, Miss Bond?"

"What for, sir?" she asked.

At this point the conversation lapsed.

At any rate the behaviour of Victorian play-goers gave Gilbert some excuse for protecting his actresses from their attentions, and we may un-reservedly accept Jessie Bond's statement that "no breath of scandal" ever touched the Savoy Theatre while he was responsible for its morals.

Sullivan had very little to do with the morals of the Savoy Theatre; in fact he scarcely came into touch with the artists at all. The music rehearsals were taken by the musical director, Cellier, and as a rule Sullivan did not put in an appearance until the dress-rehearsals, though he always went to the theatre in order to play over the songs, as each was completed, to the actors concerned. The company did not like him so much as Gilbert. He was courteous, but not so friendly; and here again they provide a strong contrast, Gilbert's popularity with his company being as considerable as Sulli-van's popularity in society. Many acts of generosity to individual artists have been placed to Sullivan's credit; yet somehow they remained indifferent to him. He did not trouble to charm them, and his interests were not theirs. He copied Gilbert's form of humour, but as it was the expression of Gilbert's character it did not come naturally from Sullivan. Though accompanied by a most attractive smile, his remarks seemed comparatively crude. Yet, according to Grossmith, who was frequently to be seen in the best society and was therefore on friendly terms with the composer, Sullivan was "brimful of humour." Grossmith gives an example. He was playing Bunthorne in *Patience* and suffering terribly from face-ache; his left cheek was so swollen that it resembled a small pumpkin. Between the acts Sullivan came to his dressing-room to express sympathy: "I'm so sorry to hear you are in such pain." Grossmith replied that he did not mind the pain, but felt that he looked an awful sight. "Not at all, my dear G. G.," said Sullivan with his usual winning smile, "I assure you it is a *great* improvement. You never looked better."

Sullivan was an adept at that form of humour. After a performance of *The Mikado* one of the "Three Little Maids" confessed to him that she had not done herself justice. "Nonsense, my dear, everybody said you were charming and didn't look sixteen," were Sullivan's soothing words. "Oh, how lovely!" she exclaimed. "No, you looked twenty-six," continued Sir Arthur.

His chaff was of the same order. "G. G.," he

remarked to Grossmith, while strolling in the enclosure at Ascot, "if it is not impertinent, how much do you pay the people who pass by you to say 'There's Grossmith!'?" A singer who thought he knew better than Sullivan how a certain song should be rendered was rebuked in these terms: "In future I'll get you to sing my songs first, then I'll compose them afterwards." A neater example of his humour is reported by Rutland Barrington, whose treatment of other people's tunes was individual and peculiar. Having accompanied Barrington right through a song, Sullivan remarked: "Very good tune indeed, Barrington, but now we'll have mine." Gilbert capped this after the first performance of an opera, when someone pointed out that Barrington had for a wonder sung all his songs in tune. "Oh, I know that first-night nervousness," said Gilbert, "it soon wears off." But the humorous side of Sullivan's nature was best expressed in sheer nonsense, as was the case with so many Victorians, and the most characteristic specimen of it is to be found in a postscript to one of his letters, which starts off with a number of complicated and indecipherable hieroglyphics and ends with the phrase: "This of course is between ourselves."

Sullivan maintained that there was no such thing as humour in music, which accounts for the unique success of the Savoy collaboration. Had he perceived the possibilities of humour in music he could not have illustrated the humour of Gilbert's words, for he would have demanded a far greater freedom than Gilbert's libretti gave him. Failing in imagination, he triumphed in interpretation. Mozart would have submerged Gilbert; Sullivan helped to keep him afloat. "We always saw eye-to-eye," said Gilbert; "the same humour always struck us in exactly the same way. With Sullivan I never had to do that fatal thing—explain a joke." Sullivan was aware that his best light music would never have been written but for Gilbert, that in some obscure way Gilbert "called the tune," and the knowledge troubled him. It made him feel only half a man, and he would try his hardest to believe that he had put his real self into his serious work. "I think this is the best thing I've done, don't you?" he anxiously enquired of Ethel Smyth, presenting her with the full score of *The Golden Legend*. Truth compelled her to say that *The Mikado* was his masterpiece. "Oh, you wretch!" he cried, and though he laughed she could see that he was disappointed. All the same, struggle against the conviction as he might, he knew in his heart that Gilbert had struck the richest vein in him, and when he was not preoccupied with his position as a serious composer he thought quite highly of his operatic work. Once a young Australian woman came to him with a letter of introduction. He received her politely, but he was clearly bored by the prospect of having to hear her sing.

"What would you like to sing me?" he asked with a sigh.

"Is there anything in particular?" she wanted to know.

"No. One thing's as good as another."

She obliged with *Ah! Fors è lui.*

"Yes, Mrs. Armstrong. That is all right." Her face fell. "Quite all right," he went on; "and if you go on studying for another year, there might be some chance that we could give you a small part in *The Mikado.*"

The young Australian woman was later to be known as Madame Melba.

Though Gilbert realised the enormous value of Sullivan's contribution, he did not fully appreciate it. He used to say that he only knew two tunes: one was *God save the Queen* and the other wasn't. The truth is that he did not much care for music, and really disliked grand opera, confessing "I would rather hear *Annie Laurie* sung with feeling than the greatest singer in the world declaiming a scene from *Tristan und Isolde.*" He was the first comic-opera librettist to achieve equality of standing with the composer. The librettist had to adapt his words and rhythms to music already written by Offenbach, for example. But with

Gilbert and Sullivan the positions were reversed, and though Sullivan might sometimes say: "My dear fellow, I can't make anything of this," and Gilbert would re-write a song to meet the objection, the composer was always the disciple, the librettist the master.

Considering their failure to form a friendship, due to their dissimilar tastes and natures, it is remarkable that they were able to work together so harmoniously. Gradually, as we shall see, their business association was undermined by the artificiality of their social relationship, but the surface of their dealings was seldom ruffled by any public display of irritation or disagreement. Occasionally Gilbert became a little restive when Sullivan was late with his songs. An instance may be given. As a rule Sullivan's settings were rapturously applauded by the company when he played them over at rehearsal for the first time, and he was a trifle nettled when one of them was received by the weary singers without enthusiasm shortly before the date of production. So he asked Gilbert for his opinion. "My dear fellow," said Gilbert, "I know nothing about music. I can't tell the difference between *Rule Britannia* and *Pop Goes the Weasel*. I merely know that there is composition and decomposition—in other words rot—and that's what your tune is!"

2

The last six months of the year 1884 were spent by Gilbert in writing, re-writing, polishing and re-polishing *The Mikado*, and since it could not be ready for production until the following spring, the Savoy was kept open after the withdrawal of *Princess Ida* with the successful revival of *Trial by Jury* and *The Sorcerer*, for which a few new numbers were written. Sullivan suffered a slight set-back in his career of fame at the beginning of '84, when the Committee of the Birmingham Festival passed him over and appointed Richter as conductor. He was extremely annoyed and expressed himself freely on the subject, asserting continually that native talent should be encouraged and that the choice of a foreigner, however distinguished, was unpatriotic. However, he forgot his griefs in a round of visits to eminent people, and throughout the season he was to be seen at Ascot, Sandown, Newmarket and other haunts of the English aristocracy. He had many friends among the members of the Jockey Club, and not only betted heavily at all the big meetings, but owned several racehorses during his years of prosperity.

In November he dined with Gilbert, went through as much of the new libretto as had been completed, and made a few suggestions. Among other things he wanted to know why Gilbert had not used any of the distinctive class titles of Old Japan. Gilbert replied that when he found the aristocracy of Old Japan were called "Samurai", the obvious rhyming phrase had decided him to keep clear of historical accuracy.

Sullivan started to write the music just before Christmas, working all night when time began to press, and the score was finished a week before the production. The rehearsals were exceptionally trying for the actors, especially George Grossmith. Gilbert had determined to make up for the comparative failure of *Princess Ida*, and he believed that a play's success was largely due to good production. He drilled the company until they were exhausted, and then drilled them again. Every step, every gesture, every expression, every inflection was rehearsed and rehearsed until the players achieved automatic exactitude. The effect on Grossmith, a highly sensitive man, was disastrous. He was reduced to a pitiable state of nervous trepidation and almost wrecked the piece on the first night. Though Gilbert can hardly be held responsible for Grossmith's nerves, it was partly due to the extreme methods of the producer that the actor took to drugs in order to keep himself going; and at the end of his long engagement at the Savoy Theatre a member of the company was horrified by the sight of Grossmith's punctured arms.

Grossmith was not the only person who suffered

from nerves on the opening night of each new production. Gilbert, who had combined the patience
of Job with the discipline of a sergeant-major
throughout the rehearsals, behaved like a frightened
child on the evening of the first performance.
Wrought up to the highest pitch of excitement and
dread, he went from dressing-room to dressing-
room, wishing the actors good luck, asking them how
they felt, reminding them of points he had already
stressed a hundred times, wondering whether they
were sure of their words, begging them to do their
best, and making a general nuisance of himself.
Then he had a last look round the stage, fussed
over the scenery and properties, and worried the
life out of the stage-manager. The moment the
curtain went up he left the theatre and wandered
about the streets in a condition of indescribable
anxiety until eleven o'clock struck, when he returned
to the theatre to hear the result and to take his bow
before the curtain. "What I suffered during those
hours," he once admitted, "no man can tell. I have
spent them at the club; I once went to a theatre
alone to see a play; I have walked up and down
the street; but no matter where I was, agony and
apprehension possessed me." Strangely enough,
he never saw his productions after the final dress-
rehearsal, and with a single exception he never
witnessed any of his operas as a member of the
audience.

Sullivan's first-night demeanour was quite different from Gilbert's, but then the tumultuous applause with which his appearance in the orchestra was always received must have given him assurance. The moment the audience caught sight of the dapper little figure, moving to his seat with quick step and cocksure carriage, the cheers broke out and sometimes lasted for more than a minute. His manner as a conductor was not spectacular. He kept his eyes on the music and his beat was restrained and cramped, the baton moving across the top or up and down the sides of the score. He wore glasses, and people sitting near him observed that the fingers of his well-manicured right hand were stained with nicotine. In spite of his unimpressive manner, he was in complete command of his orchestra and nothing escaped his attention. Once, to prove that he could be as dramatic as anyone, he altered his style of conducting, using whirlwind beats, stamping his feet, jerking his head and twisting his body. Though many people considered it a great improvement, he did not repeat the experiment.

At the conclusion of the performance the theatre resounded with cheers, applause, the thunder of beating feet, and loud cries of "author," "composer," "Gilbert" and "Sullivan." The contrast between the tall martial figure of Gilbert and the short tubby figure of Sullivan, as they came before

Richard D'Oyly Carte by 'Spy'.

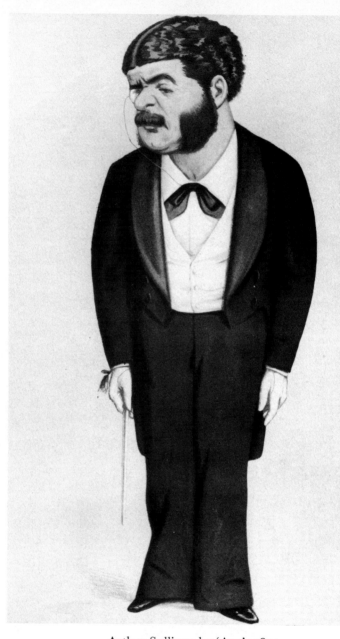

Arthur Sullivan by 'Ape', 1894.

William Gilbert by 'Spy'; *Vanity Fair*, May, 1881.

William Schwenck Gilbert.

Arthur Seymour Sullivan.

Arthur Sullivan; from the painting by Millais.

William Gilbert and his wife

'Our Artist's notes of Messrs. Gilbert and Sullivan's New Comic Opera "Patience", at The Opera Comique'. *Illustrated London News*, 1881.

Productions of well-loved Gilbert and Sullivan operas, in the 1920s: *Top left* 'Iolanthe'; *Top right* 'Ruddigore'; *Above* 'Yeomen of the Guard'.

the curtain, was heightened by their difference in bearing. Sullivan bowed gracefully, smiled affably and walked on and off the stage with ease and self-assurance. Gilbert almost had to be dragged on, scowled at the audience, inclined his head ungraciously, and seemed to resent the occasion as a personal indignity.

The Mikado was produced on March 14th, 1885, and ran for nearly two years. It was the greatest success of the series and still remains the most popular of the Gilbert and Sullivan operas. It carried the fame of the collaborators all over America, Australia and South Africa, and even aroused the enthusiasm of Amsterdam and Berlin. But it has been depreciated in the most unexpected quarters and its career of half a century has not been devoid of storms. Queen Victoria thought its plot "rather silly," and in the year 1935 a certain doctor of Boston, U.S.A., protested against its performance on the ground that it was immoral, revolutionary and obscene. During the original run the Japanese ambassador tried to have it suppressed because it ridiculed the Emperor of Japan, and a projected revival in 1907 was actually banned for much the same reason. Such opinions and episodes are of little interest and no importance. But we who are concerned with the nature of the man, Gilbert, may find something of interest and importance in the libretto of *The Mikado*, because it contains two features which are consistently present throughout his work, which clearly denote certain qualities in himself, and for which he has been harshly attacked by Sir Arthur Quiller-Couch.

"Gilbert," says Sir Arthur, "had a baddish streak or two in him; and one in particular which was not only baddish but so thoroughly caddish that no critic can ignore or, in my belief, extenuate it. The man, to summarize, was essentially cruel, and delighted in cruelty." We have already noted this feature of his work in the *Bab Ballads*, and it persists throughout his operas, though less vigorously, the classical example being in *The Mikado*:

> The criminal cried, as he dropped him down,
>   In a state of wild alarm—
> With a frightful, frantic, fearful frown,
>   I bared my big right arm.
> I seized him by his little pig-tail,
>   And on his knees fell he,
>   As he squirmed and struggled,
>   And gurgled and guggled,
> I drew my snickersnee!
>   Oh, never shall I
>   Forget the cry,
>   Or the shriek that shriekèd he,
>   As I gnashed my teeth,
>   When from its sheath
> I drew my snickersnee!

It may be said, and no doubt will be said, that all this kind of thing is the high-spirited fun and amusing nonsense of a healthy and humorous man. But when a man's work, from youth to age, is full of the entertainment to be extracted from torture, capital punishment, boiling oil, decapitation and so on, it is permissible to wonder whether a joke may not be repeated too often, whether the fun does not become less funny, and whether the humour is so very amusing or the high-spiritedness so very healthy. Mr. G. K. Chesterton has commented on the fact that Gilbert seemed to have missed the point of his jokes when he transferred them from the *Bab Ballads* to the operas. But the truth is that he could not see them in quite the same way, and here we have the explanation of their existence. When Gilbert wrote the *Bab Ballads* he had not achieved that dominion over others, the desire for which sprang from the core of his being. When he wrote the operas he had worked off a great deal of his superfluous energy in the production of plays, in quarrels, law-suits, hobbies, and in his twenty years of soldiering; also he had won a big position for himself in the theatre and could command his companies as Napoleon had commanded his armies. The cruelty that he had masked with comedy in the *Bab Ballads* merely expressed the thwarted vitality of a born man of action, who inflicted imaginary punishments on all who opposed him.

F

Though he never attained the full power of his secret desire, the more he was able to impose his will on others, the less did he express the need of domination in the fictional form of cruelty.

For we must be careful to draw a distinction between fanciful cruelty and actual cruelty. The first expresses a hidden desire, not necessarily a sadistic one, except in the sense that love of power is sadistic; though Gilbert used his power on the whole benevolently. The second is bestial and malevolent. Sir Arthur Quiller-Couch has failed to observe this distinction in his indictment of Gilbert. Yet compared with the average sportsman Gilbert was a soft-hearted humanitarian. For all his longing to be a despot, he had no real malevolence in him at all. He adored children and animals and could not bear the infliction of pain on either. "Deer-stalking," he once said, "would be a very fine sport if only the deer had guns." And when William Archer mentioned the theory that the fox enjoyed his little run with the hounds, Gilbert broke in: "I should like to hear the fox on that point. The time will no doubt come when the 'sport' of the present day will be regarded very much as we regard the Spanish bull-fight or the bear-baiting of our ancestors." He was not a fanatic on the subject of taking life, but he could not outrage his own sensibilities. To understand his nature we must contrast the figurative cruelty in his poems with the following personal confession: "I have a constitutional objection to taking life in any form. I don't think I ever wittingly killed a black-beetle. It is not humanity on my part. I am perfectly willing that other people should kill things for my comfort and advantage. But the mechanism of life is so wonderful that I shrink from stopping its action. To tread on a black-beetle would be to me like crushing a watch of complex and exquisite workmanship."

The second feature of Gilbert's work which arouses the horror of Sir Arthur Quiller-Couch is notably present throughout the operas. "But Gilbert's cruelty," says Sir Arthur, "took an uglier twist upon one incurable and unforgivable vice— that of exposing women to public derision on the stage just because they are growing old and losing their beauty . . . What disgusts one in Gilbert, from the beginning to the end, is his insistence on the physical odiousness of any woman growing old . . . Gilbert shouts it, mocks it, apes with it, spits upon it." Further, Sir Arthur states that Gilbert "opens with this dirty trump card in *Trial by Jury* . . . and so he proceeds until the end, in *The Mountebanks*, to a scene which almost drove one from the theatre in nausea."

Here again we are faced with a purely fanciful form of cruelty. Its persistence in Gilbert's work proves that it had some relation to his personality, but it cannot be taken at its face value as an indication of brutal hostility on the writer's part to ageing ladies. No normal man feels disgust at the sight of an elderly woman or the thought of a girl growing old, and Gilbert was a reasonably normal man. He was always falling in love with pretty women, and right up to the end of his life would half-humorously complain of the havoc they made of his heart. But his sense of propriety kept his behaviour within bounds, and for a man of his overbearing nature and superabundant vitality the self-imposed restraint had to show itself in other directions. His emotions, dammed at their true source, burst forth into unexpected channels; and it is a tenable theory that his strong moral inhibitions, acting upon his keen susceptibility to female beauty, produced an acute state of dissatisfaction, which he revenged upon the less attractive members of the sex. The fact that he never ridicules an elderly man in love with a young woman, a much commoner spectacle than the one he usually derides, strengthens the supposition. This perverseness, and not the easy superficial view that he was a cad, would explain his otherwise inhuman onslaughts upon spinsters of an uncertain age.

In the affairs of everyday life his impulses were constantly at war with his respectability, and the victory of the latter was shown in his antipathy to handsome men, whose advantages placed them in a better strategical position and seemed to release them, in some curious way, from moral responsibility. Quarrels on specific points apart, his frequent brusqueness with men arose from his sense of their greater freedom in these matters. It often happened that he was not on speaking terms with friends and acquaintances for years together. At the Beefsteak Club, where the other members called one another either by their Christian names or by nicknames, he was always addressed as "Gilbert"; and once, on entering a room, he was heard to exclaim in surprise: "A dozen men, and I'm on terms with them all!"

Perhaps the worst example of his rudeness was due, not only to the cause already indicated, but also to his hatred of female effusiveness, particularly about music.

"Oh, Mr. Gilbert, please tell me the name of that *won*derful thing they are playing now," gushed a woman who was suffering from a bad attack of spots on the face.

"I think," answered Gilbert, his eyes riveted to her pimples, "I think it is *La Petite Vérole*."

"Oh, Mr. Gilbert, you are so very droll!" she squeaked with pleasure, and went off to tell everyone how very droll he was.

3

So pronounced was the success of *The Mikado* that

there was no need for the partners to think of their next opera for some time to come. Gilbert settled down quietly to enjoy his new house in Harrington Gardens, which became the scene of marvellous children's parties, when the host would stuff them with sweets, load them with presents, take the lead in their games, and behave like Santa Claus and Mr. Maskelyne rolled into one. Yachting and tennis occupied most of his time in the summer, and he was a regular playgoer when the days shortened, but he was not very fond of dining out, preferring to entertain a few carefully selected friends in his own home, when he would relate amusing stories in a dry quiet voice or flirt with the prettiest woman present, telling his wife when she laughingly protested that he was "too good to be true." Though he enjoyed his meals, he declared that it was not so much what was on the table as on the chairs that mattered. People attached too much importance to the business of feeding. "My cook gets eighty pounds a year and gives me a kipper," he said; "Sullivan's cook gets five hundred pounds a year for giving him the same thing in French." But he was annoyed when someone invited him to a poor meal and threatened to "pay him out by asking him to dinner. I have an avenging sherry at one and nine which I think will astonish his digestion."

Sullivan's life was not so well ordered as Gilbert's. In the summer of '85 he tore himself away from the tables of the great and crossed the Atlantic. His brother's widow had recently died and he had made himself responsible for the children, who were now left to look after themselves at Los Angeles, where the family had settled shortly after the death of Sullivan's mother. The reason for his visit to America was therefore a personal one, but he was not allowed to pass through the continent unheralded. In New York he tried but failed to escape the reporters, who discovered his hotel and cornered him in his apartment. In Chicago he made an effort to shake them off by starting to remove his clothes the moment he reached his bedroom, but they would not stand on ceremony and interviewed him in his shirt and trousers. He visited Salt Lake City, saw the Brigham Young family, played on the organ of the great Tabernacle, went to a service and heard one of his hymn-tunes. At San Francisco there was a plague of reporters. With the assistance of a detective he gave them the slip one evening and visited Chinatown, going into "the vilest dens," but life in the hotel was unendurable because of the swarm of folk who descended upon him the moment they caught a glimpse of him in room or corridor, and he fled to Los Angeles, where he found his nephews and nieces and transported them at once to the Yosemite Valley, where there was not much likelihood of meeting a newspaper representative.

Having settled his family affairs, he returned by easy stages across the continent, receiving municipal honours in some towns, passing unknown through others. At one place his reception was peculiar.

"How much do you weigh?" asked a prominent citizen.

"One hundred and sixty-two pounds," he answered in amazement.

"Hell!" said the prominent citizen.

It turned out that they were expecting a boxer named "Slogger" Sullivan, but when it was discovered that his name was Arthur one of them wanted to know whether he was "the man as put *Pinafore* together." On receiving confirmation of the fact, the prominent citizen said: "Let's have a drink."

September saw him back in New York, where Carte's production of *The Mikado* was playing to full houses and a pirated production at another theatre was not doing so well. They celebrated his presence in the city with a gala performance whereat Sullivan, in a speech, suggested that the American Government might give the same legal protection to a man who used his brains in writing or composition as to one who invented a new beer-tap. After producing *The Mikado* in Philadelphia with Carte's assistance he sailed for England in October.

He found the country Mikado-mad.   From

drawing-rooms, concert-halls, cottages, street-corners, came the well-known airs. Queen Victoria strummed them, barrel-organs murdered them, business-men hummed them, errand-boys whistled them, and the future Kaiser wrote to tell Sullivan that as soon as he could get rid of "a very serious and rather dangerous attack of ear-ache" he would attend a performance in Berlin. Sullivan felt that he could rest on his laurels, but Gilbert felt otherwise, for he wrote to say that they must now get to work on "the (as it seems to me) admirable plot I proposed to you last year"—in other words, the lozenge plot. Sullivan was seriously disturbed over the reappearance of the fatal lozenge and wrote to Gilbert begging him to forget all about it. Gilbert could not forget all about it, but he laid it aside for a stormy day and concentrated on something else. One January morning in 1886 he walked through a blizzard to Sullivan's flat (it must have reminded them both of the first reading of *Trial by Jury*), and after Sullivan had helped to relieve him of the snow that lay in drifts on his overcoat they went through the plot of *Ruddigore* together. Sullivan was pleased with it, and they sketched out the whole story, but he told Gilbert that he would have to write a work for the Leeds Festival before starting on the new opera. Gilbert received the information with fortitude and they parted amicably.

A wave of laziness now overtook Sullivan, and

F*

though he had given Joseph Bennett three hundred pounds for a libretto founded on Longfellow's *Golden Legend* he could not settle down to composition. Instead he went to race-meetings, introduced Liszt to London society, and hobnobbed with the nobility. By April he had done nothing and was recalled to duty by Gilbert, who cursed him for being idle and received the reply: "Do you take me for a barrel-organ?" He rented a cottage at Yorktown and began *The Golden Legend* a few weeks later, but work progressed slowly at first. May went by and he had done scarcely anything. June came and still the effort was "awfully tedious." July found him absorbed at last and for six or seven weeks he hardly went out of doors. He was in pain at regular intervals throughout the entire composition and towards the end, when the mental strain was increasing his bodily infirmity, he hardly enjoyed an hour free from suffering.

The Golden Legend was performed at the Leeds Festival on October 15th, 1886, and was received with delirious enthusiasm. The audience yelled themselves hoarse and pelted him with flowers. He turned to bow his acknowledgments to the choir, who also pelted him with flowers. The newspapers agreed with the audience and choir. *The World* called him "the Mozart of England," and said that, though it was difficult to claim a place in the foremost ranks of composers for the author of *The*

Pirates of Penzance, the case of the author of *The Golden Legend* rested on a very different basis.   It still does.

The plaudits had not ceased to ring in his ears when Gilbert wrote to congratulate him on what "appears from all accounts to be the biggest thing you've done" and to remind him that the music for *Ruddigore* had still to be composed.   Sullivan now balanced his period of laziness earlier in the year with one of extreme activity.   In spite of the fact that he was preparing performances of *The Golden Legend* for the Albert Hall, Queen's Hall, Crystal Palace and St. James's Hall, he started on the new opera and wrote some of his best music for it.   Each collaborator had a high opinion of his own contribution to *Ruddigore* and was not too pleased with the work of the other.   Yet such was their curious relationship that they dared not express their feelings frankly to one another but tried to influence their friends to do it for them.

"How do you think the piece is shaping?" Sullivan asked a man who was on friendly terms with them both.   "It is supposed to be an opera, but it is really becoming a play with a few songs and some concerted music.   Don't you think it would be as well to hint to Gilbert that the music is disappearing in the background?"

"Though to my uninstructed ear," Gilbert said to the same friend, "nothing could be better than the music, there is so much of it that I am afraid the audience will lose the thread of the story and forget what it is all about. Perhaps you could suggest to Sullivan that if one or two numbers were cut the piece would play more briskly."

The story was founded on an early sketch of Gilbert's, and of course he made use of one or two ballads, but the whole piece was put together with considerable skill, and it is certainly one of his best libretti. After the unparalleled success of *The Mikado* he was most anxious to maintain the Savoy standard of achievement, and for this purpose he allowed certain friends to witness the later rehearsals in order that he might benefit by their criticisms. The company resented the indignity of being taught their business before people they did not know, and one day Rutland Barrington gave voice to their discontent:

"I refuse to rehearse before a row of stalls filled with strangers," said he.

Gilbert was naturally furious at this public rebuke, and the company trembled as he worked off his emotions in appropriate speech. Having relieved himself of the momentary irritation, he realised that the actors had a reasonable grievance and the stalls were emptied of their occupants. But he did not overlook Barrington's presumption, and for several days after the incident he said to any member of the company who happened to be watching a rehearsal from the stalls:

"You mustn't sit here; Barrington won't like it."

Ruddigore was produced on January 22nd, 1887, and went very well up to the last twenty minutes of the performance, when the audience became restless. At the fall of the curtain the first "Boo" in the history of Gilbert and Sullivan opera was heard from the gallery. Whether this expressed the general feeling that the sailor's song about "the darned Mounseer" was a slight on the British navy, or the popular objection to the resurrection of the ghosts, it is difficult to say. It may have come directly from a "darned Mounseer," since Gilbert received several challenges to duels from Frenchmen who felt their country had been insulted. At any rate, the opinion of the audience and the critics was that the new work was not half so good as *The Mikado*, and many people took exception to the title. This annoyed Gilbert, who suggested that it should be changed to *Kensington Gore*: or *Not Half so Good as The Mikado*.

The morning after the production the partners met at Sullivan's flat and made a number of alterations and excisions; next day they changed the Finale, so that the ghosts remained spectral; but when a play receives a mixed reception on the first night, no amount of titivation can make a success of it, and the run of *Ruddigore* only just beat that of *Princess Ida*. It was what the Savoy partners called a failure: that is to say, Gilbert made seven thousand pounds out of the original run, Sullivan made more because of the sale of his music, and Carte made most because, having only financed instead of creating it, he naturally made most.

Of course there were recriminations. Sullivan thought that by bringing the ghosts back to life Gilbert had ruined the piece. Gilbert thought that Sullivan had not treated the ghost scene humorously enough. "I fancy he thought his professional position demanded something grander and more impressive than the words suggested," said Gilbert, adding that the ghost music was like introducing fifty lines of *Paradise Lost* into a farcical comedy. These opinions, however, were not exchanged by the partners, who were content to whisper them into the ears of their friends.

Gilbert was always a little touchy about *Ruddigore*. He felt, rightly, that it contained some of his finest work, and he was quick to resent the least intimation that it failed at any point. Some years after its production, George Edwardes, who had been Carte's manager at the Savoy Theatre and whose musical comedies at the Gaiety Theatre started a new fashion in light entertainment, declared in a newspaper interview that "Mr. Gilbert used to polish his work to the minutest degree, and then he would absolutely refuse to have it altered in any way . . . I think that sometimes Mr. Gilbert would have found it better to alter and experiment.

This might have saved a fine work like *Ruddigore*."

This remark did not save Edwardes from Gilbert, who wasted no time in polishing his rejoinder: "Mr. Edwardes is quite right in supposing that (after polishing up my work to the minutest degree) I have not been in the habit of handing it over to a stage-manager to embellish with alterations and additions at his good pleasure. If I had done so the Savoy pieces would, no doubt, have borne a stronger resemblance to the productions with which Mr. Edwardes' name is associated, but that was not the object I had in view."

Gilbert remained sensitive, not only about the opera, but its title, which had been described as coarse and unseemly. Meeting a friend in the street one day, the conversation suddenly took a personal turn.

"How's bloodygore going?" asked his friend.

"You mean *Ruddigore*," corrected Gilbert.

"Same thing," said the other.

"Indeed?" returned Gilbert acidly. "Then if I say I admire your ruddy countenance (which I do), it means I like your bloody cheek (which I don't)."

4

The mixed reception of their new opera had a mixed effect on the two partners. Sullivan was again at the mercy of his solemn mentors, who did not fail to point out that now was the time to break away from the Savoy and compose works more worthy of his genius. Gilbert, who had satisfied his lust for writing works more worthy of his genius at an earlier period, was now solely concerned with the problem of increasing his investments. The result was that Sullivan went abroad to ponder on mightier themes, while Gilbert remained at home and reconsidered the possibilities of the lozenge.

Having sustained an earthquake at Monte Carlo, Sullivan went on to Naples, where he was laid up with a grave attack of the disease that cast an ever-lengthening shadow over his life. By March he had sufficiently recovered to attend the celebrations of the Emperor William's ninetieth birthday at Berlin and to conduct *The Golden Legend* at the Opera House. The Prince of Wales and many other royalties had gathered together to honour the Emperor, and Sullivan spent a good deal of time in their company. Owing to the complete failure of the soloists to rise to the occasion, the performance of *The Golden Legend* was a disaster, and Sullivan obtained permission from the Court to arrange another. Madame Albani rushed to his rescue from Antwerp; the royal family were again present; and the second performance was a triumph. Wherever he went during his stay in Berlin regimental bands played selections from *The Mikado*, and altogether he was able to congratulate himself on the honours that were heaped upon him.

Back in England he learned that *Ruddigore* might not last out the summer, and Gilbert and Carte called to talk matters over. To his dismay Gilbert at once plunged into the lozenge plot and declared that it alone could save the situation. Sullivan, his mind on higher things, agreed to reconsider it when part of it was written, but extracted a promise from Gilbert that, if it did not appeal to him then, the subject should be dropped. The trio resolved to revive past successes until a new piece should be ready.

Gilbert retired to his house at Uxbridge and got his teeth into the lozenge, writing in a few weeks to report progress. By that time Sullivan was worrying over an Ode by Tennyson, for which the Prince of Wales had asked him to write the music. This was to be played in June at the laying of the foundation stone of the Imperial Institute by Queen Victoria, whose Golden Jubilee was being celebrated. Sullivan had some difficulty with the Ode, writing it, destroying what he had written, and trying again. Eventually he managed to do the entire composition in a four-hour sitting. "It met with universal approbation," the Prince of Wales wrote to him, "and the Queen was specially delighted with it."

Meanwhile Gilbert, unaffected by royal jubilees, was absorbing his lozenge, and early in September he read the scenario to Sullivan, who objected to its lack of human and dramatic interest and declined to write the music for it. Gilbert again pigeon-holed the plot, but stated, flatly and finally, that hé had no intension of thinking out another, hoping perhaps that his attitude would bring Sullivan to his senses. It did nothing of the kind. For many weeks Sullivan had been fighting his disease; he had no patience to spare for Gilbert; and it was during this period of estrangement that an ominous incident occurred at the Savoy. One day D'Oyly Carte chaffed Gilbert about the condition of the carpet outside the door of the room which he shared with Sullivan. It was shabby; it had a hole in it; surely, said Carte, a man who was earning such colossal royalties as Gilbert ought to spare a few shillings for his mat. Gilbert, who hated chaff and usually scented some malicious motive behind it, flared up at once and retorted that as Sullivan earned more than double his own royalties, music being considered of *much* greater value than libretti, it was up to him to get a new piece of carpet. At that moment Sullivan appeared, feeling very much below par, and what started with a joke ended in a violent controversy.

Once more the clouds lifted. After several weeks in bed with a recurrence of his malady, Sullivan went to the Savoy to conduct a music-rehearsal of *Pinafore*, which was the first of the revivals that had been decided upon. There, by accident, he met Gilbert, whose business-sense had begun to function again and who had thought of an entirely fresh plot which he was going to call *The Tower of London*. Sullivan was immensely relieved. A little later Gilbert spoke of the play as *The Tower Warden*, later still as *The Beefeater*, finally as *The Yeomen of the Guard*. Sullivan did not mind what it was called so long as it was not about a lozenge.

The idea for the new plot had come to Gilbert when waiting for a train at Uxbridge station, where he had seen a poster of a beefeater. Soon the story took shape in his mind, and fortunately it made an instant appeal to Sullivan, because it was human and free from topsy-turveydom. Sullivan, the dreamer, was always crying for reality. Gilbert, the realist, was always crying for dreams. But on this occasion the desires of both were appeased, for Gilbert contrived to dress his dream in the costume of reality. He spent days in the Tower of London and thoroughly enjoyed writing a work which he always declared to be his best opera. He put a great deal of what he thought was his essential self into the character of "Jack Point," and regarded this idealised Gilbert as a greater creation than any of Shakespeare's jesters. He was never happier in his partnership with Sullivan than when he was engrossed in this plain tale of the Tower, for it was the nearest he ever got to the Gilbert of the earlier plays, the poet he imagined himself to be. It was therefore a terrible shock to him when Sullivan wrote from Monte Carlo that, after mature reflection, he had decided to abandon comic-opera and devote himself henceforth to serious work.

Having left the impression that he was delighted with the new work, Sullivan had gone to Algiers and the South of France early in '88. There he meditated upon various matters; the persistent warnings of his friends, Grove and Macfarren, the constant friction with Gilbert, the periodical resurgence of the lozenge, the illness which was growing upon him and making work on anything but the most exalted subjects burdensome to him; above all, the extraordinary success of Cellier's comic-opera *Dorothy*, which had already passed its five hundredth performance at the new Lyric Theatre. This last achievement made him feel thoroughly uncomfortable. It seemed that inferior composers could make fortunes out of comic-operas. So why should he, Arthur Sullivan, debase his art merely in order to compete with people whose success could equal his own? The thought rankled, and in the disquietude of his soul he determined to dedicate himself to the nobler forms of music, in which he felt that he excelled.

Gilbert gasped. Was Sullivan going mad? Did he really think *The Golden Legend* was a better work than *Ruddigore*? Did he believe that he could live in comfort on serious music? What did the success of *Dorothy* matter? Damn *Dorothy*! Had not *The*

Mikado run for two years? Had other musicians stopped composing because of its success? The company at the Savoy was the best in England; the composer was the best in England; the librettist was of course the best in England; Gilbert and Sullivan Opera was a national institution, like Westminster Abbey; and did Sullivan seriously intend to wreck the whole business and sacrifice a gold mine merely because rubbish like *Dorothy* could fill a theatre for five hundred nights?

Gilbert committed these reflections to paper and sent them off to Sullivan, advising him at the same time, since it was possible a run of bad luck at the tables had affected his brain, that he ought to try Gilbert's system: "Back red until it turns up twice in succession, then back black till it turns up twice— then back red and so on. I tried it a dozen times . . . and always won." Possibly the tip for the tables was successful, possibly he went down heavily on it and as a consequence the "gold mine" argument in Gilbert's letter became operative; at any rate Sullivan was convinced, and when he returned to London he showed his disinclination to religious music by plunging into the social life of the capital. He did, however, conduct a command performance of *The Golden Legend* at the Albert Hall, when Queen Victoria earned the gratitude of serious music-lovers by telling him that he ought to write a grand opera. "You would do it so well," she said.

Although they were again working in harmony, Sullivan's attempt to break up the partnership had upset Gilbert, who betrayed his irritation in affairs unrelated to its cause. One day Grossmith brought him a message from a young actor who was anxious to play the leading part in a forthcoming revival.

"He only wants you to give him the first refusal of the part," added Grossmith hurriedly.

"With the greatest pleasure," came the unexpected reply.

"That's very kind of you," murmured Grossmith gratefully.

"Not at all," said Gilbert; "I refuse him at once."

A far deeper sense of dissatisfaction came for a moment to the surface when Sullivan, quite within his rights, refused to lend the Savoy Theatre for a few matinées of *Broken Hearts* which Gilbert wished to revive with Jessie Bond in the leading part. Sullivan based his refusal on the ground that if the theatre were used for the purpose of "starring" one member of the company there would be no end of applications from other members of the company who wished to be "starred"; and as the theatre could not be lent without the permission of all three partners, his objection settled the question. Nothing illuminates more clearly the chasm that divided the partners than a letter written by Gilbert to Jessie Bond, in which he complained bitterly of

Sullivan's "unwarrantable and ill-advised" action. He told her that Sullivan had not consulted him about lending the theatre to the College of Music, but had assumed that as a matter of courtesy he would raise no objection. "Next year, however, it may be otherwise," was the minatory postscript.

A revival of *The Pirates of Penzance* succeeded that of *Pinafore* in March '88, to be followed by *The Mikado* in June. Sullivan went to Fleet in Hampshire at the conclusion of the social season and started on *The Yeomen of the Guard*, which was put into rehearsal during August. He wanted Gilbert to make a number of alterations. Gilbert protested, but eventually agreed; and while Sullivan was staying with the Empress Eugénie at Farnborough or playing poker in the summer residences of his wealthy friends, Gilbert was reconstructing the second act. With the first breezes of autumn Sullivan began to make up for lost time, and during September he worked all through the nights, seldom turning in before six a.m. He experienced considerable difficulty over the setting of *I have a Song to Sing O* and tried in vain for a fortnight to get the right tune. Gilbert offered to recast it, but he was so pleased with it as it stood that he would not allow it to be altered. At last he gave it up in despair and said to Gilbert:

"You often have some old air in your mind which prompts the metre of your songs; if anything prompted you in this one, hum it to me—it may help me."

This was quite true, because Gilbert frequently achieved a particular rhythm with the aid of a tune he had heard, but as a rule Sullivan would say: "Don't tell me what the tune is, or I shan't be able to get it out of my head." However, the present situation was desperate, and though, as Gilbert said, "only a rash man ever asks me to hum," he did his best to reproduce the air of a sea chanty that the sailors on his yacht used to sing in the "dog-watch" on Saturday evenings. He had not hummed a dozen bars before Sullivan exclaimed:

"That will do—I've got it!"

Gilbert wondered whether his humming had proved too much for Sullivan, whose sudden exclamation might have been a cry of pain. But Sullivan assured him that for once he was responsible for the music as well as the words.

The Yeomen of the Guard was produced on October 3rd, 1888, and was given such a tumultous welcome that Sullivan thought its success would be greater than that of *The Mikado*. Right up to the last moment Gilbert was the victim of nervous apprehension. The commencement of the opera was in his opinion too serious; he had warned Sullivan about it again and again; and on the morning of October 3rd he wrote to his collaborator "to place upon record the conviction" that the play's success would be seriously imperilled unless certain musical numbers were shortened or withdrawn, adding, lest Sullivan's vanity should be hurt, "I am proposing to cut, not only your music, but my words." A few minutes before the curtain went up they reached a compromise, and then Gilbert started his regular first-night fuss. Jessie Bond as "Phoebe" (alone on the stage at the rise of the curtain) was almost driven crazy by his questioning. "Are you sure you're all right, Jessie?" "You haven't forgotten anything?" "Mind and take the keys from Denny at the right moment." "Are you feeling nervous?" "Remember that——" but Jessie had had enough. "For heaven's sake, Mr. Gilbert, go away and leave me alone, or I shan't be able to sing a note!" He gave her a last frenzied hug, dashed from the stage, vanished from the theatre, and tried to stem his agitation for the next three hours in the streets.

The papers were lavish with praise the next day, and by a coincidence Sullivan received a letter that morning from the Duke of Edinburgh, who enclosed a decoration from the Sultan of Turkey "as a mark of his appreciation." In making a request for selections from the operas the Duke said that the favourite piece played by the band on board H.M.S. *Alexandra* was Sullivan's music to *Henry VIII.* Sullivan had also written music for three other plays by Shakespeare, *The Tempest,*

The Merchant of Venice and *The Merry Wives of Windsor*, and now in October '88 he was approached by Sir Henry Irving to provide the music for the Lyceum production of *Macbeth*. Irving had a very vague idea of music, but he knew what sorts of sounds he wanted, and he gave Sullivan a brief outline of his requirements: trumpets here, drums there, a march at this point, a flourish at that, and one player at rehearsals "to tootle tootle," so that they could hear the exact tunes. Apparently the player did not always "tootle tootle" the kind of thing Irving had in his head, and an interesting fact emerges from this brief union. Just as Gilbert, by a most unmusical humming, was able to inspire Sullivan with the tune for a song in *The Yeomen of the Guard*, so did Irving, by an exercise in cacophony, obtain from Sullivan the very themes that he needed. The company watched entranced as their chief stalked the stage, swaying his body, moving his arms in curious convolutions, now making strange croaking sounds in his throat, now tapping his feet on the boards to keep time with the moaning modulations that issued from his lungs.

"Much better than mine, Irving, much better," Sullivan would cry the instant he perceived what the other was trying to express; "I'll rough it out at once." And when the orchestra played the new version, based on the actor's startling exhibition, it was always exactly what Irving wanted.

Here is another proof that Sullivan was the

perfect medium. He could transmit the essence of words (or even croaks) into music; but, being of an essentially feminine nature, his best work was only produced under the spell of a dominating and masculine personality—Gilbert, as it happened, though it might have been Irving. The strong feminine strain in him appealed intensely to the equally strong motherly instinct in Ellen Terry, who wrote to him after the production of *Macbeth*: "It was *lovely* to have you at the theatre."

Both Gilbert and Sullivan thought that *The Yeomen of the Guard* was their finest work together. The general public did not agree with them, and the general public were right. It is a serious opera, and owing to the restrained nature of their relationship seriousness did not become them. Their happiest combination was on the plane of facetiousness. They flirted together in perfect accord; and since a misunderstanding invariably gives a zest to flirtation, their two best works were produced after their two biggest quarrels. Already we have seen *The Mikado* emerge from the ashes of their anger. Now we are to witness another and a greater storm, to be followed by the yet serener calm of *The Gondoliers*.

5

At the fall of the curtain on the last performance of the revival of *The Mikado*, four days before the

production of *The Yeomen of the Guard*, there had
been a great ovation for Rutland Barrington, whose
long and continuous association with the Savoy
Theatre was then brought to a close. There was
no part for him in *The Yeomen*, and he wished to
start a season of his own in "straight" plays. As he
had made his reputation in Gilbertian parts he
naturally asked Gilbert to provide him with
another for the opening of his season.   Gilbert
obliged with *Brantinghame Hall*, a curious medley of
melodrama and satire, in which the women-wor-
shipped parson reappeared in a different setting.
It was Gilbert's opinion that no man created anything worthy of himself until the age of forty.
Assuming that a man reaches the age of forty, this
is probably true; though it must also be admitted
that many men over forty create works unworthy
of themselves.   Gilbert was one of them, and
Brantinghame Hall was one of the works. It was produced at the St. James's Theatre on November
27th, 1888, and in Gilbert's own phrase, invented
on this occasion, it "failed to attract." He seems
to have been in a genial frame of mind during the
rehearsals, probably because he did not take the
play too seriously, and several of his recorded
witticisms date from this period.

"Actresses often paint, but they do not always
draw," was one of them.

When reproved by Barrington for keeping the

company waiting, he said: "I have lost more time through being punctual than through anything else."

Someone took him to task for using the word "coyful" in one of his operas. "How can anyone be full of coy?" he was asked.

"I don't know," he replied, "but for that matter how can anyone be full of bash?"

To an actress who had to cry "Stay! let me speak" at a certain point in the play, but who kept crying "Stay! stay! let me speak," he said: "It isn't 'Stay! stay!'; it's 'Stay!'—one stay, not a pair of stays."

To another actress, a very attractive one, who was going to give a special performance at Brighton and who said that she would have to take her mother with her as chaperon, he remarked: "Couldn't you trust the old lady in town for *one* evening by herself?"

At that time a well-known manager, who was supposed to be living with a certain actress, had cast her for a leading part and was puffing her in the press. Gilbert's comment was: "The fellow is blowing his own strumpet."

Barrington's solid manner was of course an excellent foil to Gilbert's quips, and with less responsibility on his shoulders than usual the producer amused himself at the expense of the actor.

"Where's Miss Blank?" enquired Gilbert at the conclusion of an act.

Barrington, who was sitting with him in the stalls,

pointed to the door leading through to the stage and said: "She's round behind."

"I know," said Gilbert, "but where is she?"

While the players at the St. James's Theatre were being entertained by Gilbert, matters of greater moment were engaging the mind of Sir Arthur Sullivan, who delivered an address on Music in the Town Hall, Birmingham, towards the end of 1888. One passage in it concerns us, because it explains the popularity of his serious music among the Victorians and also his limitations:

"Herein lies one of the divine attributes of music, in that it is absolutely free from the power of suggesting anything immoral. Its countless moods and richly varied forms suit it to any organisation, and it can convey every meaning except one—an impure one. Music can suggest no improper thought, and herein may be claimed its superiority over painting and sculpture; both of which may, and, indeed, do at times, depict and suggest impurity. This blemish, however, does not enter into music; sounds alone . . . must, from their indefinite nature, be innocent. Let us thank God that we have one elevating and ennobling influence in the world which can never, never lose its purity and beauty."

We could perhaps follow his meaning more closely if he had provided a definition of the word "impurity." But in any case his views might have been modified if he had talked over the subject with Wagner or Tolstoy. The truth is that Sullivan had by this time absorbed the Victorian belief that sex and art should be kept in separate moral-tight compartments. His favourite contemporary authors were Bret Harte, Conan Doyle, Stanley Weyman and Anthony Hope. "In fiction," he confessed, "I must say that I do like what I call healthy work." In music, too, he liked what he called healthy work.

For the third of the famous Savoy partners, D'Oyly Carte, the year 1888 had been notable. He had married his secretary, Miss Lenoir, a terrific worker with exceptional business ability, and it was largely through her influence and energy that he was driven to attempt the conquest of another theatrical kingdom—that of Grand Opera—which in due time had its effect on the relationship between the three men.

Sullivan, as we know, had been pining for fresh fields, and Queen Victoria's hint had resolved his ambition. Even his solemn counsellors had praised *The Yeomen*, but simply with the object of furthering their plans for his future. It was a step in the right direction; now, surely, he must see for himself that it would be madness to stop short of grand opera. Sullivan agreed, especially as it would liberate him from Gilbert, whom he was beginning to regard as his evil genius, talking openly of his work at the

Savoy as "this slavery." His resolution was formed and his plans were made by the New Year, and when, early in January '89, Gilbert called to discuss business, he commenced to outline his intentions before the other could get the lozenge off his chest. He expressed his determination to abandon light opera and undertake some serious dramatic work on a large scale, in which the music should be all-important and the composer should have the final word. Knowing quite well that the feeling would not be reciprocated, he said that he would like Gilbert to do the work with him. Gilbert was so taken aback by his partner's purposeful manner that all he could do was to nod his head in seeming assent.

A few weeks later Sullivan defined his intentions more clearly in a letter and felt he was quite safe in hoping once more that Gilbert would collaborate. But during the interval Gilbert had been thinking things over. He had no desire whatever to write the libretto for a grand opera, still less to play second fiddle to the composer. He was convinced that there was no public for English grand opera. *The Yeomen*, their most serious work, was not repeating the success of *Patience*, *Iolanthe* or *Pinafore*, to say nothing of *The Mikado*. Also he did not fancy the site whereon Carte was building an opera house, and he thought that Sullivan would have great difficulty in getting together a cast of good singers who could act. Such were the opinions he put forward in a letter to his partner, adding that there was no reason why Sullivan's serious compositions should conflict with his work on light opera. Why could he not do both? For Gilbert professed to understand and sympathise with Sullivan's desire "to write what, for want of a better term, I suppose we must call Grand Opera."

Sullivan was at Monte Carlo when this letter arrived. He had recently been staying with the Prince and Princess of Wales at Sandringham, had then accompanied the Prince to the Continent, and was now enjoying princely festivities on the Riviera. His regular visits to the tables were reported in the papers, and he was extremely annoyed when certain English journals commented on his heavy gambling. What with dining among lords and counting his losses, he was in no mood to discuss grand opera with Gilbert. But he wrote again, recapitulating his main objections to Gilbertian comic opera: he was tired of it; his work was too good for it; he did not want to spend the rest of his life in clothing the same old types with music, e.g. "the middle-aged woman with fading charms"; he disliked the inhuman and impossible plots; in fact, the whole business had become distasteful to him. To Gilbert's assertion that in serious opera the librettist would be sacrificed, he retorted that he had sacrificed himself in every single one of the

G

comic operas they had written together. Having said which, he left it to Gilbert to find a way out of the *impasse*.

Gilbert's reply was brief and pointed: if Sullivan really imagined that he had been effacing himself during the last twelve years, and if he was seriously proposing that for the future Gilbert should efface himself, there was nothing more to be said. "If we meet, it must be as master and master."

When Sullivan read this letter all the pent-up irritation and resentment of twelve years burst forth, and there was something curiously womanish about the way in which his emotions, once released, got the better of him, turning the main issue into a series of disconnected accusations and personal grievances. It was also rather feminine of him to unbosom himself, not to Gilbert, whose fearful scowl and withering comment kept him in awe even at a distance, but to a sympathetic third party—*the* third party. In his letter to Carte he accused Gilbert of ignoring his suggestions, of wasting everybody's time at rehearsals, of ruining his music, of treating his opinions with contempt, of tiring the actors so that they sang out of tune, of rudeness, egotism, domineering and bullying. Summarising the situation in a phrase, he wrote: "I am a cipher in the theatre."

Having relieved himself of the grievances he had nursed for more than a decade, his mood changed, and the letter he wrote to Gilbert the day after he had posted his bitter epistle to Carte was pitched in a different key. It was almost apologetic in tone, as if he were afraid that he had gone too far, as if he wished to break the force of the coming blow. Why should they quarrel, he asked, about a matter that could so easily be arranged? All that he desired was that he should have more to say in the purely musical part of their operas, that his judgment should weigh with Gilbert "in the laying out of the *musical situation*." That granted, and it seemed a rational request, there was no reason why they should not continue their successful partnership.

Only a few weeks before, he had talked soberly and definitely about his future in serious music and his abandonment of comic opera. Now he was almost begging for a continuance of their collaboration. Obviously he did not quite know what he wanted to do; but of one thing he was certain. His rash letter to Carte would infuriate Gilbert, and it suddenly dawned upon him that he could not face the future without Gilbert. Serious music was all very well, but one could not live on it; still less could one gamble on it; and Sullivan was now to reap what he had sown. Social life among the butterflies of Mayfair and Ascot had become second nature to him. To flutter in those exciting circles he had to compromise. He would write his grand opera; but his income was only secure at the Savoy; backing Gilbert he was on "a cert."

The next move came from Carte, who forwarded Sullivan's letter to Gilbert. It is a little difficult to divine Carte's motive for doing so, since he must have known that Gilbert was not the man to read it with the detachment of a Chesterfield and that it would probably result in the break-up of the partnership. Possibly he was too sanguine of the success of his new venture which he hoped to commence with a grand opera by Sullivan. Possibly he felt that the letter would terminate the constant friction between the partners and lead to an amicable understanding. But it is more probable, as we shall find later, that he believed Sullivan to be the real money-maker at the Savoy and that so long as Sir Arthur continued to write the music the box-office receipts would not vary. Such a belief satisfied him in a double sense, for he was devoted to Sullivan, but disliked Gilbert's autocratic manner and interfering ways. The fact remains that, whether actuated by policy or pique, he sent the letter to Gilbert.

Breakfast that morning in Harrington Gardens must have been a difficult meal to digest. Gilbert received the two letters by the same post. The one from Sullivan was written in a more friendly strain than he had expected; in fact he was merely being asked to do what he had always done; he had never failed to meet Sullivan's requirements. But the enclosure from Carte maddened him. What on earth did Sullivan mean? A more grotesque fabrication of baseless accusations he had never read. The letter was cruel, unjust, ungenerous, libellous, monstrous. Had he not always given in to Sullivan? Had not Sullivan's every whim been unhesitatingly gratified? Had he not deferred to Sullivan again and again? Had he not been the acme of reasonableness?

These reproaches were expanded and set forth in a long letter to Sullivan, which concluded with the statement that if a man of his unequalled position in the world of music really had submitted in silence for twelve years to the slights of which he complained, then it was not upon Gilbert that the charge reflected but upon himself.

The intensely masculine element in Gilbert's nature is shown in his immediate reaction to Sullivan's complaints. Their long collaboration had been the union of opposites; socially an ideal union if they had been man and woman, a perpetual discord since they were man and man. On the plane of art this discord ceased and the primary elements in their natures fused to a perfect concord. Their essential dissimilarity was never so clearly displayed as at this moment of their lives. We sympathise with Sullivan's sense of injury, for he had always given in to his partner and was always angry with himself for having done so. We understand

Gilbert's incredulous astonishment at the outburst, for he had always been most anxious to agree with Sullivan, so long as Sullivan agreed with him.

Gilbert's letter followed Sullivan to Venice, whither he had gone after a period of utter boredom at Monte Carlo. "I am tired of the eternal gambling and the jargon connected with it," he had written to a friend, "and the people don't interest me." He was a man who quickly tired of doing anything for long, and his sudden impulse to visit Venice was merely an attempt to distract his mind from a different form of mental distraction. All through the month of April a spate of letters passed between the two. The burden of Gilbert's was that he had always considered Sullivan's interests, and the burden of Sullivan's was that his interests had never been considered. It did them a lot of good to get rid of their annoyance on paper, and after the first fortnight each of them began to climb down, since neither wished to shatter an alliance that had brought them fame and fortune. Inside a month they had reached the "Be this as it may" stage of their argument, and it was Sullivan who terminated the quarrel with the statement that he was willing to write another opera with Gilbert at once; though, with a sudden memory of the lozenge, he added in parenthesis that they should be in thorough agreement as to the subject.

Letters had also been passing between Carte and

Sullivan, in which the manager, with an eye to a break in the partnership, had pressed the composer to write a serious opera ("Grand Opera is an offensive term," said Sullivan to placate Gilbert) for the opening production at the new theatre. Sullivan was delighted at the prospect of achieving the ambition of his life, especially as he could choose his subject and his collaborator, and agreed to have the opera ready by the following spring. This meant that he and Gilbert would have to start work immediately on the next piece for the Savoy.

Early in May they met in London, had a long frank discussion, and, in Sullivan's words, "shook hands and buried the hatchet." A month later Gilbert arrived with the story of *The Gondoliers*, which Sullivan thought "funny and very pretty." For five months Gilbert worked on the libretto, sending the songs as each was completed to Sullivan. Both of them were out of town, Gilbert at Uxbridge, Sullivan at Grove House (now Bridge House), Weybridge, and their correspondence during this period was of the friendliest description, each trying to give more than he took. Indeed, the atmosphere following the last upheaval was so calm that it seemed to presage another storm.

George Grossmith left the Savoy during the run of *The Yeomen*, and Rutland Barrington was returning for *The Gondoliers* after his disastrous season at the St. James's Theatre; but as Gilbert had experienced trouble with his leading artists, all of whom had asked for a rise in salary commensurate with their rise in fame, he decided to have no "star" parts in the new opera. Jessie Bond, however, declined to appear in the next piece unless her salary were raised from twenty pounds to thirty pounds a week. When Gilbert heard this he wrote to tell her that, in spite of his high appreciation of her merits and his personal affection for herself, he had to consider his partners, and under no circumstances would he consent to the extra ten pounds. Jessie persisted, Sullivan and Carte supported her, and Gilbert had to give way. Not, however, with a good grace, for he never spoke to her at rehearsals, only acknowledging her presence as she came on the stage with a remark addressed to the other members of the company:

"Make way for the high-salaried artiste!"

Gilbert was not ungenerous, but he hated being beaten, and on this occasion his partners, whose interests he was guarding as well as his own, sided against him. For a man of his temperament it was a bitter pill to swallow, and it took him some time to recover. But he bore no malice against Jessie Bond, for after the dress-rehearsal he rushed up to her, kissed her in front of everyone and cried:

"Jessie, my dear! I had no idea that so much could be made of so small a part!"

Rehearsals began in the middle of October, and

all through November Sullivan worked hard every night. He resembled Gilbert in one respect, and one only. Neither could stand interruption when seriously at work, and therefore both preferred to work at night time. With their previous operas Gilbert had usually managed to send off the entire libretto ("Here goes what may be worth five pence or five figures," he would say as he posted it), but this time Sullivan received it in small portions, and the score gave him more trouble than any of its predecessors. He appears indeed to have plagiarised Molloy's *Love's Sweet Song* in his *When a Maiden Marries*, but when taxed on the subject he replied: "I don't happen ever to have heard the song, but if I had you must remember that Molloy and I had only seven notes to work on between us."

Gilbert allowed his brain to run away with him in the original script, and only five days before the production of the piece he agreed with Sullivan that some "dangerous dialogue" should be cut out. But nothing could now save Gilbert in the eyes of officialdom. He had been too critical of the professional buttresses of the State, and his very irresponsibility, the fact that he did not represent Socialism or any other "ism," but mocked at every class and every creed, made him still more dangerous, because it meant, surely, that he was an anarchist disguised as a Tory. However, his impertinence was about to be punished. He had dared to

G*

flout Authority, and Authority was now going to show that it could ignore him. Authority, in fact, had decided that he did not exist, in the belief, presumably, that his non-existence would teach him a lesson; and when a Command Performance of *The Gondoliers* was given before Queen Victoria at Windsor Castle his name was omitted from the programme, though the name of the wig-maker was printed in bold type.

The opening performance, on December 7th, 1889, was the most brilliant of all their first-nights. At the close they received an ovation that could be heard outside, above the roar of the Strand. It was, with *The Mikado*, the greatest success of their joint career, and on the whole it remains their most delightful work. The libretto was the wittiest Gilbert ever wrote, and the music caught its spirit to perfection. It was written in a period of emotional tranquillity, of which they were keenly conscious because of its harsh prelude, and to which some foreboding of the coming strife may have lent an especial grace.

In writing to thank Sullivan for the splendid work he had done, Gilbert said: "It gives one the chance of shining right through the twentieth century with a reflected light."

"Don't talk of reflected light," Sullivan answered. "In such a perfect book as *The Gondoliers* you shine with an individual brilliancy which no other writer can hope to attain."

6

Within a month of their triumph at the Savoy, Gilbert was enjoying a holiday in India and Sullivan was back at Monte Carlo. On his return home in March Gilbert received from Carte an account of the preliminary expenses in connection with *The Gondoliers* and saw to his amazement that the total was four thousand five hundred pounds. He wrote for details, and discovered that Carte had included the sum of five hundred pounds for new carpets for the auditorium. Gilbert had already had a little trouble with Carte over carpets, and he was annoyed that the manager should have calmly taken the matter into his own hands and charged the sum to production expenses. Besides, by their agreement with Carte, Gilbert and Sullivan were only liable for "repairs incidental to the performance," and if carpets for the lobbies and staircases came under that heading, then they were also responsible for repainting, decorating, reseating, lighting, and everything else that was done to the theatre. Gilbert wrote to Carte, drawing his attention to these facts and stating that he should have been consulted before the carpets were bought. Carte's reply was so extraordinary that we can only assume he meant to enrage Gilbert. He said that both Sullivan and himself were tired of the perpetual interference of Gilbert in matters that did not concern him, and that if this kind of thing continued he (Carte) and Sullivan would have to look for another librettist.*

This letter was a spark to the gunpowder in Gilbert, and he exploded. His future actions must be judged in reference to its insulting terms. He had been the dynamic force behind the partnership; to his methods as a producer, no less than to his ability as a writer, the greatest success in stage history was due; he could claim that but for him Carte would not be the wealthiest man in the theatrical world. And now he was plainly being told that his services could be dispensed with.

There was a stormy interview, in which the business argument was interspersed with volleys of expletives: "D'you think I'm going to pay for a confounded carpet for the stairs to an office where you do the dirty business of your blasted opera house, you blankety-blank?" Such undiplomatic language poured from Gilbert, and it is hardly surprising that they failed to reach an understanding.

Sullivan was home again in April, and Gilbert went to see him. They discussed the various points at issue, and as Sullivan did not entirely see eye-to-

---

* Since this highly significant letter, mentioned here for the first time, explains Gilbert's later attitude I must state that my authority for it is Mr. Jack Robertson, an Old Savoyard, to whom Gilbert showed it at Grim's Dyke. In company with his fellow artists Mr. Robertson had a high regard for Gilbert's character and genius, and strongly resented the terms of the letter.

eye with Gilbert he promised to arrange a meeting
between themselves and Carte in order to go over
the whole subject in dispute, Gilbert himself suggesting that no reference should be made to his recent
angry scene with Carte. Next day Gilbert called
again, read the headings of a new contract which he
proposed all three should immediately sign, and
agreed with Sullivan that the atmosphere would be
less electric if the meeting of the trio were postponed
for a week. A few days later Sullivan wrote to
Gilbert that, though he thought they should have a
fresh contract, there was no need to draw it up
until a new piece was wanted for the Savoy. Gilbert felt that Sullivan was letting him down, and at
once despatched a letter to Carte, notifying him
that he was not to produce or perform any of
Gilbert's libretti after Christmas, 1890, and a note
to Sullivan, stating that their collaboration was at
an end and that *The Gondoliers* would be the last of
their works to be heard in public.

This brought Sullivan and Carte to their senses.
Carte wished to cripple but not kill the goose that
laid the golden eggs. Sullivan, though tired of
Gilbert's fractiousness, was anxious for peace while
writing his grand opera. They therefore proposed a
meeting of the partners in Carte's office. Gilbert
accepted their invitation, but the sight of Sullivan
in the enemy's camp was too much for him, and
the meeting did not pass off according to plan. The

arguments of the other two were wasted on him.

"The expenses are unwarrantable and excessive," he stormed at Carte, "and I demand a fresh agreement, because you are making too much money out of my brains."

Carte continued to argue, while Gilbert sat glowering. Suddenly Gilbert turned to Sullivan and demanded his opinion. Without hesitation Sullivan sided with Carte. Gilbert instantly saw red.

"You are no gentlemen," he shouted, "or you should answer to me. You are both blackguards!"

He then let loose a torrent of abuse that shocked Carte and hurt Sullivan, rushed at the door, wrenched it open, and bellowed a threat:

"I'll beat you yet—you bloody sheenies!"

The door banged, the atmosphere lifted, and the two remaining members of the firm breathed freely.

Many people who lose their sense of proportion in a fit of excitement are cautious enough to delay further action until they have slept on the subject that caused the fit. But one night's rest was not enough for Gilbert. He should have gone to bed for a month after every row. Though able to wake up and rub his eyes in a peaceful frame of mind, by the time he was fastening his collar the sense of injury had begun to operate, and within an hour he had again reached boiling point. On the morning after his distressing scene with Sullivan and

Carte he sat down and wrote to the former, demanding (1) an apology for his hostile attitude the previous day, and (2) a severance of his connection with Carte; failing both of which Gilbert insisted on dissolving their partnership. Sullivan refused to comply, and said that Gilbert had not behaved like a gentleman.

Thus the dissolution of their union, which had lasted for thirteen years, resulted immediately from the fact that neither of them considered the other a gentleman. Without enquiring too closely into the meaning of the word "gentleman," on which point gentlemen never agree, we know now that the real cause of quarrel between these two had nothing whatever to do with conventional standards of behaviour. People do not quarrel because they happen to disagree on certain matters, however serious—an atheist can live in perfect concord with a Christian—but because they are not in harmony with one another, because their characters clash. Enough has already been said about the basic division between the characters of Gilbert and Sullivan, which was the root cause of the trouble. Had they liked one another better, had they been capable of warming towards one another by virtue of a single common inclination, the Savoy partnership would have lasted until Sullivan's death.

The immediate, but superficial, cause of quarrel was due, firstly, to Carte's carpet. Carte was an

extremely shrewd man of business, and there are
very few shrewd men of business who would not
take advantage of an ambiguous phrase in a contract. Even so it may be thought that, under the
onslaught of Gilbert, he would have given way.
But Carte fancied himself as a sort of Napoleon
(his photo shows a hand thrust imperially between
the buttons of the coat), and Gilbert's dictatorial
methods had got on his nerves. Success had gone
to his head and he was suffering from that last
infirmity of business minds—a belief that he knew
exactly what the public wanted. His Moscow lay
ahead, in the form of grand opera at the superb new
theatre he was building, but when the carpet
question was at issue he had a settled conviction
that he and Sullivan could afford to laugh at Gilbert's libretti, and incidentally make their author
eat the pie of humility.

The reason for Gilbert's behaviour is only too
clear. Carte's contemptuous letter followed by
Sullivan's treachery, as he thought it, would have
goaded a much less sensitive man to an outburst of
ungovernable fury; though here again, had he
really cared for Sullivan, he would have sympathised with the composer's predicament. As it
was, all that he could see was the defection of a
fellow artist, the betrayal of their common cause by
a man who with himself had helped to fatten the
financier, an artist deserting another artist and

selling himself to an accountant. Add to the letter
and the treachery a severe attack of gout, and we
need seek no further reason for his contribution to
the dispute.

But while Gilbert was trying to beat the business
man at his own game, Sullivan was forced to join
with the business man for the sake of his fame. The
ambition of his life was about to be realised with
the help of Carte. The words "Grand Opera"
blazed across his spiritual horizon. He could not
throw away this wonderful chance merely for the
price of a carpet. And what a trifle to make a song
about! He had lost sums like that in one evening at
the Monte Carlo tables. Gilbert was being altogether too troublesome. He could not everlastingly
be at war with Gilbert and fighting his kidney
disease; it was too tiring. Had he felt the least
affection for Gilbert, he would have tried to see
the situation from the other's angle, he would have
explained his own difficulty, he would have offered
to pay the five hundred pounds himself, he would
have aroused Gilbert's quickly touched sympathy.
As it was, he decided that Gilbert was not a gentleman.

Gilbert was a born fighter. Firmly believing that
in every dispute he was right and the other fellow
wrong, he went to extreme limits to prove his rectitude. A century earlier he would have fought at
least one duel a week, and it was only his contempt

for lawyers that prevented him from taking legal action as often as he had a quarrel. In temper and in temperament he was like Hotspur, and in business dealings he would have echoed that choleric warrior:

> But in the way of bargain, mark ye me,
> I'll cavil on the ninth part of a hair.

To be beaten ("cheated" was his word) in a business deal was worse than the gout; he felt mentally crippled; and he would try any cure, even the law, in order to recover his self-esteem. Characteristically, when suffering badly from gout, he called one of his swollen feet "Labouchere," after the editor of *Truth* who had made cutting comments on him, and the other "Clement Scott," after the dramatic critic of *The Daily Telegraph* who had also been unpleasant; and he took a "vicious pleasure (not unalloyed with pain)" in cramming "Labouchere" into a boot which was much too small for him. Unfortunately he was suffering from gout-at-the-feet and carpet-on-the-brain during the months that succeeded the quarrel, and the two complaints resulted in a correspondence with his late partners which, if it could be recovered, would furnish an ideal text-book on the art of abuse. Sullivan wrote to a friend in June that he would have attended a certain concert, "but I had a combined attack that day, my old physical trouble and . . . Gilbert!"

In August, with *The Gondoliers* running to packed houses, the general public were astonished to read in the papers that Gilbert had made an application for the appointment of a receiver at the Savoy Theatre and that he was bringing an action against Carte and Sullivan. The case was adjourned for a week, when it came before a vacation judge, and another adjournment was applied for on the ground that Gilbert was ill at Carlsbad. Counsel for defendants protested against "the cruel manner" in which the case was being allowed to stand over. However, the judge granted a further postponement and the case was finally heard in the first week of September. It appeared that Carte received four thousand pounds per annum for the rent of the theatre and necessary expenses. After deducting this, the profits were divided equally between the partners, though each had to pay his share of the production expenses. It was Carte's duty to render an account and pay out the profits at the end of each quarter, but owing to the disagreement over the April account Carte had not made the usual quarterly payment in July, his solicitors informing Gilbert that it would be better to settle the earlier account before any further sums were paid. Gilbert had promptly issued a writ for settlement of the July account. Carte's solicitors had then sent him a cheque for two thousand pounds, but Gilbert had claimed (on the strength of the nightly takings) that at least three thousand pounds was due, and had applied for the appointment of a receiver. For the defendants it was stated that Gilbert's share of the net profits of the eight operas that had been produced during the past eleven years had been seventy thousand pounds for London and twenty thousand pounds for America and the provinces, and that pending the action Carte ought not to be called upon to render any further account; also that the appointment of a receiver at the Savoy Theatre would be prejudicial to the interests of all concerned. The case having been fully argued, it was finally arranged that Carte should make Gilbert a further payment of one thousand pounds on the following day and should deliver the July account within three weeks, paying any balance due to Gilbert for that quarter within four days of delivery.

Gilbert had triumphed and was so pleased about it that he wrote to Sullivan suggesting a truce with Carte. Sullivan replied that he was "still smarting" from Gilbert's treatment of him, that he was "physically and mentally ill over this wretched business," and that if confidence between them were to be restored Gilbert would have to admit that he had been in the wrong. Gilbert took two months to accustom himself to the feeling that he

might have been a little less precipitate, but in
November he called on Carte, admitted that
the gout had got the better of him and discussed
the carpet in a spirit of compromise.

All this time Sullivan had been composing his
grand opera, trying hard to keep his mind busy
with romantic themes while violent letters from
Gilbert were arriving at Weybridge with mortifying frequency. The subject he had chosen was
Ivanhoe, and his taste for "healthy" romantic literature was very evident in the choice. Ever since the
production of *Princess Ida* he had longed for the
opportunity of dealing with a grand historical
theme, and *Ivanhoe* provided him with all the satisfactory ingredients: the novel was healthy, romantic,
popular, moral and clean. Yet the music did not
come easily at first. He wrote and destroyed and
re-wrote, never retaining anything that he did not
deem worthy of the subject. It was to be his greatest
contribution to music, and he put his life's blood
into it. Fortunately he could not know that the
only song in it that would achieve anything ap-
proaching the popularity of his Savoy numbers,
Ho Jolly Jenkin, was the one song in the work that
might just as easily have appeared in any of his
comic operas.

A double cast was engaged, and no expense was
spared in the production. Staged with every
imaginable effect of scenic splendour, it was

performed for the first time at the opening of the
Royal English Opera House (now the Palace
Theatre) on January 31st, 1891, before an audience
that included the Prince and Princess of Wales, the
Duke and Duchess of Edinburgh, sundry other
royalties, and the pick of London society. Gilbert
was not present. "I decline your stalls," he wrote
on the morning of the 31st, and followed up his
refusal with two more letters on the same day. The
opera was received with tremendous enthusiasm,
the English language was ransacked for eulogistic
adjectives by the critics, and Queen Victoria expressed "particular satisfaction, . . . as she believes
it is partly owing to her own instigation that you
undertook this great work." Sullivan confessed
that the opera had been directly inspired by Her
Majesty and dedicated the music to her. A fortnight later Gilbert consented to sit through it, but
in spite of the fact that he was not bored ("the
highest compliment I ever paid a grand opera"),
Ivanhoe was only performed a hundred and sixty
times. Sullivan was deeply disappointed, as he
had hoped it would run as long as a successful piece
at the Savoy, and being of an extremely impressible
nature, its failure lessened his own opinion of the
work.

"I like it," said a young composer, hoping to
encourage him.

"That's more than I do," answered Sullivan; "a cobbler should stick to his last."

On hearing that Sullivan was dissatisfied with his diminishing royalties, Gilbert remarked:

"He's the sort of man who will sit on a fire and then complain that his bottom is burning."

From which we may guess that Gilbert still harboured a grievance. He could not shake off "a dull leaden feeling" that Sullivan had treated him "with inexplicable unfairness," and early in October '91 Chappell, the music publisher, acted as ambassador between them. Gilbert believed that they would never be able to meet again if either of them had a grievance against the other, and he suggested that they should refer the whole dispute to a third party, whose decision would settle it finally and enforce an admission from one of the disputants that he had been in the wrong. Sullivan could not bear the thought of raking up the whole business; he wanted to forget it, and was ready to meet Gilbert in the most friendly spirit on condition that the quarrel was never referred to. On October 12th they met, talked for two hours, shook hands heartily and parted friends, or as near to friendship as they were ever likely to get.

Prior to this reconciliation Gilbert had been busy on a new comic opera. It is perhaps unnecessary to add that, with Sullivan safely out of the way, he had resuscitated the lozenge. Lots of young composers wrote to offer their services. To one of them he granted an interview.

"You're very young, Mr. de Koven," he said, after staring at the youth for about five minutes.

"That's a matter time will cure," replied de Koven, getting up and taking his leave.

Another wrote from Australia, begging for a chance to display his talent and stating: "Though by profession a chemist, I am a born musician."

Gilbert replied: "I should prefer to collaborate with a born chemist who is a musician by profession."

Having chosen Alfred Cellier to write the music, he approached several of the Savoy company with tempting offers to leave Carte and Sullivan and act in his new piece. One of them accepted, but when Sullivan got to hear that Gilbert was trying to inveigle Jessie Bond from the Savoy he wrote and implored her not to leave. Carte's letter suggesting an increase in salary was more to the point, and she stayed with the old firm. It should be added that the company as a whole sided with Gilbert in the famous quarrel, not because they knew anything about it, but because they liked him better than Sullivan.

A year after Sullivan had attained the ambition of his life with the production of *Ivanhoe*, Gilbert's perseverance with the lozenge was rewarded by the production of *The Mountebanks* at the Lyric

Theatre (4th January, 1892). The libretto was quite as good as any but the best of his Savoy pieces, and it was more successful than any opera composed by Sullivan apart from Gilbert, but with the passage of time the lozenge had somehow been diluted and Gilbert seemed to have lost his taste for it; at least the plot no longer hinges upon it. The song "Put a Penny in the Slot" affirms his ineradicable faith in the corruptibility of all mankind, and the subject of decaying females again engages his attention. This time, after taking the liquid (erstwhile lozenge), a pretty girl turns into the old hag she is pretending to be in a play; and when she breaks the news to her lover that her age is real and not the excellent make-up that he is praising, she adds distressfully: "Of course, you won't love your little woman now!" To which he replies: "I shall have much pleasure in—in showing you every attention compatible with the—the respect due to a lady of your advanced years, my—my pet!" Gilbert's lifelong distaste for "star" actors, especially tragedians, comes out in the passage he puts in the mouth of a mummer: "I've played the first acts— and the first alone—of all our tragedies. No human eye has seen me in the second act of anything! My last appearance was three months agone. I played the Moody Dane. As no one else had ever played him, so I played that Dane. Gods! how they laughed! I see them now—I hear their ribald roars. The whole house rocked with laughter. I've a soul that cannot brook contempt. 'Laugh on!' I said, 'laugh on, and laugh your fill—you laugh your last! No man shall ever laugh at me again—I'll be a clown!' I kept my word—they laugh at me no more."

While *The Mountebanks* was doing good business at the Lyric, Sullivan was at Monte Carlo trying to compose the music for a libretto by Sydney Grundy. A recurrence of his disease in the early part of '92 nearly killed him. For weeks he lay semi-conscious, his pain deadened by repeated injections of morphia. He thought he was dying and in the intervals of consciousness made arrangements for that event. Sometimes he would snatch a few minutes, free from morphia and pain, and work feverishly on the new opera. Then a paroxysm of agony would seize him and for hours together he was under the influence of the drug. The news spread that he was sinking. The Queen sent a telegram, the Prince of Wales sent a surgeon. But it was doubtful whether he could survive an operation. One day his nephew, with the help of his valet, gave him a hot bath. It did him more good than the ministrations of the physicians, and from that moment he began to mend. He was brought back to London and gradually recovered in the June sunshine, driving about the Parks, visiting Lord's, and staying at Sandringham with the Prince and Princess of Wales. By

August he was again composing, with the result that *Haddon Hall*, the music for which had been written between spasms of agony or in the feebleness of convalescence, was produced at the Savoy on September 24th, 1892. Gilbert was there, and the first performance seemed to promise success for the opera. But although the music achieved barrel-organ popularity, the promise was not fulfilled, and the piece was soon withdrawn.

Carte was now beginning to question his infallibility. His grandiose scheme for English Grand Opera had come to nothing. If Sullivan had failed it was unlikely that anyone else would succeed; so he sold his new theatre to a music-hall syndicate. The failure of *Haddon Hall* was another blow. It meant that Sullivan without Gilbert was not the same as Gilbert and Sullivan; whereas the success of *The Mountebanks* proved that Gilbert without Sullivan was at least a paying proposition. Carte had already spent a lot of time in a vain attempt to find a worthy successor to Gilbert; he had discovered a young fellow named James Barrie, but Barrie's libretto had not appealed to Sullivan; later Carte was to approach a critic named Bernard Shaw, but Shaw could not preach in libretti, and nothing came of it. With *Haddon Hall* playing to half-full houses, Carte was in a fix; so he stopped looking for Gilbert's successor and tackled Gilbert himself. By the end of 1892 the three partners had thoroughly discussed the business side of a new alliance, and Gilbert and Sullivan had agreed to write their next opera together.

Sullivan was back on the Riviera for the winter months; Gilbert paid him a flying visit to discuss the plot and then set to work. Another severe attack of gout sent him limping to Homburg, but he stuck to his job and finished the piece in July. Sullivan spent the summer months composing the music at Weybridge. He was delighted to be at work on another of Gilbert's libretti. "After all, there's nobody like him," he said. But there was a certain amount of friction. Carte informed them that the production expenses would come to seven thousand pounds, and this time it was Sullivan who fought for economy. Gilbert explained that the "Gents in arms . . . must be dressed *somehow*, they can't go naked (unless you insist on it)," but Sullivan was in favour of retrenchment in every direction. Again Sullivan objected to the comical treatment of a middle-aged lady in love. Gilbert protested that middle-aged ladies in love were essentially comical, but he was forced to climb down and give the part "pathetic interest." Finally the composer objected to the Finale of Act 2. Gilbert lost patience and told Sullivan to write the music, after which he would try to fit it with words. This was the only time in their experience that such a thing had happened, and Gilbert was not too pleased about it.

"Here it is," he wrote, enclosing the verses; "it is mere doggerel, but words written to an existing tune are nearly sure to be that," and he gave Sullivan carte blanche to chop the stuff about as much as he liked. It was a hot summer, and Sullivan worked slowly, varying his labours with rides on a tricycle, rows on the river, and attendances at race-meetings.

The final dress-rehearsal of *Utopia Limited* was witnessed by critics and others. Gilbert said that the critics had attacked his previous work because they had not understood it, and he hoped that if they had an opportunity of seeing an opera twice running it would give their intelligences time to function before writing their criticisms. From his point of view he was right, for the press was almost unanimous in praise of the piece. It was produced on October 7th, 1893, and though one of the best efforts of the famous pair, it only ran for eight months. Perhaps its partial failure was due to Gilbert's criticism of English affairs: parliament, the army, the navy, commerce, the Court; this time he had given rein to his satire with a vengeance. He had not forgotten the omission of his name from the programme of the Command Performance at Windsor, and the form of his revenge gave great offence in Court circles. In those days there was a popular troupe of comedians at St. James's Hall known as the Christy Minstrels. They blackened their faces to look like niggers and were expert in the art of buffoonery. The King of Utopia holds a Cabinet Council of Englishmen who have come to show him how to run the country, and the stage-direction reads: "They range their chairs across stage like Christy Minstrels." Taking his chair, the King says: "You are not making fun of us? This is in accordance with the practice at the Court of St. James's?" To which one of his Council replies: "Well, it is in accordance with the practice at the Court of St. James's Hall."

At the close of the first performance there was great excitement. Gilbert and Sullivan took a number of "calls" separately, but the audience were not content with that, and Sullivan was quick to take advantage of the situation. While Gilbert was on the stage bowing his acknowledgments, Sullivan suddenly appeared from the wings with outstretched hand. Gilbert played up to him; they shook hands; and the audience shouted themselves hoarse while the curtain went up and down on the reconciled couple.

7

Apart altogether from those infusible elements in their characters which made them mutually anti-pathetic, something else had now crept into the relationship between Gilbert and Sullivan that rendered their continued partnership difficult to maintain. They had experienced the relief of work-ing with men to whom their word was law; they had tasted the joy of enfranchisement from the bondage of equality; and so, while writing *Utopia Limited*, they had both felt the strain of what Gilbert had once described as a "master and master" colla-boration. Carte did his utmost to bring them back to business—Sullivan from his dream of drama and romance, Gilbert from his love of lozenges and lyrics—by telling them that what people wanted was simply "fun," and plenty of it. He assured them that a modern farcical comedy set to music, with a low salary list and a cheap production, would re-establish them completely. But his re-marks fell on deaf ears. Gilbert did not want to write a modern farcical comedy, Sullivan did not want to set one to music, and both of them had made sufficient money to release them from the drudgery of doing what they did not like. They were getting on in years, could afford to pick and choose, and had no intention of submitting to the policy of give-and-take, since each was now con-vinced that he gave far more than he took

Sullivan celebrated his birthday in May '94 with a dinner at the Garrick Club, at which everyone of note in the theatrical world was present except Gilbert. Of course, the Prince of Wales and the Duke of Saxe-Coburg (formerly of Edinburgh) were there, and the dinner was followed by a reception of ambassadors, etc., at Queen's Mansions. "I shan't have any more birthdays," he said after it was over; "I am fifty-two, and it is time celebrations should cease."

Gilbert was fifty-eight that year, but he felt young enough to write and thank a friend for a present which arrived "on the eve of my twenty-fifth birthday." He remarked on the number of congratulatory letters that poured in on these occasions, complaining that "everyone always seems so glad when I'm a year older that there's no chance of my forgetting the fact. I suppose the general joy will culminate when I die."

Both of them spent a fairly lazy year, glad to be free from the necessity of providing new pieces for the Savoy. Gilbert patched up an old libretto, wrote a few new verses, and produced *His Excellency* (music by Dr. Osmond Carr) at the Lyric Theatre in October. Sullivan got Burnand to furbish up their early work, *The Contrabandista*, added some fresh music, and it appeared at the Savoy in December under the title of *The Chieftain*. He also did the incidental music for the Lyceum production of *King Arthur*. But there was no suggestion on either side that they should write another opera together, and when at the end of '95 Gilbert sent Sullivan a new libretto it is doubtful which of the two was less enthusiastic about it. However, Sullivan did his duty to Carte, and *The Grand Duke* was performed a hundred and twenty-three times at the Savoy Theatre, commencing on March 7th, 1896. It was the final flash in the pan; in fact it was only a spark; and the most famous association in theatrical history fizzled out like a damp squib.

. . . .

It is not the biographer's duty to evaluate the creative output of his subjects; his business is with human life and character; but since there has been a recent tendency to underrate the work of Gilbert and a corresponding tendency to overrate Sullivan's contribution, and as such a mental attitude ignores the human element in the collaboration, the subject must be briefly touched upon.

The modern view is neatly summarised in the course of a letter from Mr. Bernard Shaw to the author of this book:

"Sullivan has been gaining ground and Gilbert losing it since they died. The reason is that when they started Gilbert was new and unique; he had absolutely no rivals. But Sullivan was hard up against Offenbach, whose music was like champagne, and also against Auber, whose Fra Diavolo was a masterpiece. Sullivan was a church organist; and when I in my teens heard *Trial by Jury*, which stands out as Pickwick stands out in Dickens, its harmonies struck me as most unexpectedly churchy after Offenbach.

H

"Offenbach and Auber are now forgotten; and Sullivan's music is as light as air beside Elgar's or Prokovieff's.

"Besides, Sullivan's vein was never worked out: he was as good at the end as the beginning. But Gilbert, fundamentally a sentimentalist who never learnt the value of his own satire, got worked out very desperately. People used to say that the two quarrelled about a carpet, which was very silly nonsense. But when Gilbert could give Sullivan nothing better to set to music than The Darned Mounseer, Sullivan, who was always a serious musician, must have felt deeply offended in his art."

This view is of course coloured by Mr. Shaw's admiration for an art which he would like to master and indifference to an art of which he is a past master; nevertheless it expresses the modern attitude fairly accurately and has a certain transient interest, though it scarcely skims the surface of the subject. A comparison between the two men is worthless, because each was vitally necessary to the other; and even if we wish to assess their relative values, we are faced at once with the fact that neither of them has lasted on his own merits. We may say, if we like, that selections from Sullivan's music are played on every pier-head in the kingdom, while selections from Gilbert's libretti are not recited at every smoking-concert, but that is merely because people prefer tunes to rhymes, narcotics to stimulants. We may also say that Gilbert has impressed his plots, poems and personality on the common mind to such an extent that he is quoted more often than Sullivan is whistled, and that his name has received an adjectival honour granted to no one else in the language. But all this is beside the point, which is that Sullivan has not been "gaining ground" apart from Gilbert and that Gilbert has only been "losing it" apart from Sullivan.

It would no doubt be true to say that, while Gilbert was the more remarkable personality, Sullivan was the rarer artist; but it would also be true to say that, while neither can be described as great without the other, together they are unique. And here we perceive the futility of comparing their individual merits and the cause of their inseparable gift. The strength was Gilbert's, the sweetness was Sullivan's, each providing his partner with something he lacked. Gilbert kindled the fire of genius in Sullivan, whose flame irradiated Gilbert.

A quarter of a century before they joined hands, Wagner wrote a letter to Liszt, from which the following passage is taken:

"If ever a *musician* wanted *the poet* it is Berlioz
. . . He wants a poet who would completely
penetrate him, who would *conquer* him by delight,
who would be to him what man is to woman."

Sullivan also wanted that poet, and found him
in Gilbert.

CHAPTER V

I

THE last work Gilbert and Sullivan did together broke the spell of their joint reputation and destroyed the hope of a final reconciliation. It was their first undoubted failure; and as success was the only thing that made their partnership endurable, a permanent severance became inevitable. They freely criticised their respective shares in *The Grand Duke*, and that was the last straw. When Gilbert had lost Sullivan's admiration, and Sullivan had lost Gilbert's approval, there was nothing left to fall back upon. A chance word of condemnation overheard or passed on, an irritable expression noted or reported, and everything that had been unpleasant in their past association became magnified out of all proportion. Pride, jealousy, personal antipathy did the rest, and in a sort of dazed anger they parted, never to speak to one another again.

Once more Sullivan was ill. He had tried every miscalled cure, but as the years went on the disease gripped him more firmly, and the periods of ease were so rare that he seized upon them greedily, enjoying them with the abandon of one who knew that his time was short. But he had to pay for these brief bouts of pleasure, and sometimes he went to take the waters at Contrexéville, where there was "a constant delicious whirl of dullness, the counterpart of which is only to be found in England at a Y.M.C.A. weekly evening recreation." While there he had to rise at six, be massaged and douched, drink six pints of mineral water, and walk until breakfast at ten. There was nothing more to eat or drink until dinner at six in the evening, and he had to be in bed by ten o'clock. It was not exciting, and he informed a friend that the two meals were "the two great events of the day."

His illness and the final break with Gilbert made the thought of writing another light opera extremely irksome to him, and he dallied with themes for a second grand opera. Having picked on King Arthur as a suitable subject, he veered round again to comic opera, and finally decided to do the music for a ballet, *Victoria and Merrie England* (the combination did not appear to strike him as incongruous), which was to celebrate the Diamond Jubilee. His determination was a fitting prelude to his social ·ife during the next few months. In August '96 he visited the Engadine, where he spent much time in he company of the Duke and Duchess of Teck,

one of whose daughters, Princess May, gave him
"a beautiful photo of herself and the children."
Next he went to stay with the Empress Frederick of
Germany and entertained her with "all sorts of
scraps" on the piano. He spent the winter months
on the Riviera, working on the ballet and gambling
at Monte Carlo, and here he came into contact
with the subject of his musical meditations. Queen
Victoria was staying at Cimiez, and wanted him
to write a Jubilee hymn which could be sung in
every church throughout the Empire. On Easter
Sunday, 1897, he played the harmonium (by his
own request) at the chapel she attended and
received from her "a lovely pocket-book" as a
souvenir of the occasion. In fact he did everything
that could be expected of a devoted subject, though
he drew the line at setting a Jubilee effusion
by Alfred Austin, the Poet Laureate, partly no
doubt because he had temporarily abandoned
comic opera. The ballet was produced on May 25th
before an audience sprinkled with royalties and
heaving with the emotion of the moment; and on
July 5th his loyal labours were rewarded by a
dinner with the Household at Windsor, a conversation of twenty minutes with Her Majesty in the
Long Corridor, and a gift of the Jubilee Medal.

A month later he went to Bayreuth for *Parsifal*,
the "Ring" and another dose of high society. The
Prince and Princess of Wales were there, Lady

Grey, A. J. Balfour, and other lovers of serious music in comfortable surroundings with good cooking. Sullivan did not care for Wagner; he described the characters in *Rheingold* as liars, thieves and blackguards; fortunately a heavy lunch sent him to sleep during *Walküre*, with the result that he found it less dreary than the rest; he thought *Siegfried* incredibly tedious, its sublime moments swamped by "puerile drivel"; as for *Götterdämmerung*, the first act was "dull and dreary," the second "just as dull and dreary," but the third, after an interval for sustenance, seemed to him the best piece of music in the entire work. Though he once declared that the *Meistersinger* was the greatest comic opera in the world, it is obvious that his sense of humour was temporarily in abeyance, and his general view of Wagner was unfavourable. However, he made up for this by unqualified praise of less turbulent composers, and shortly after his dismal experiences at Bayreuth he acclaimed the genius of a youngster named Coleridge-Taylor, whose *Hiawatha* had much impressed him.

His failure to appreciate Wagner is not surprising. Wagner expressed his personality in music and the leit motiv in his works, which annoyed Sullivan, corresponded with the leit motiv in his life. Sullivan's personality was not dominant enough to find expression in his works and there was no leading motive in his life. His best music was the medium whereby another man's personality was expressed, though of course the complementary energy was latent in Sullivan, waiting to be harnessed to Gilbert's. But Sullivan's serious music does not express himself because, firstly, his personality was not sufficiently assertive, and, secondly, there was no governing force in his life. He lived in a permanent condition of cross purposes. He was tugged a dozen different ways. His ambition to write serious music was undermined by his fondness for society; his yearning for grand opera was at odds with his natural bent towards light opera; his wish to produce works of a religious nature was counteracted by his love of life; his craving for popularity fought his desire for fame. The ceaseless distractions of gambling, horse-racing, card-playing, travelling, good living, society-chasing, royalty-hunting, took their toll of his spiritual being, and the aspirations of his early manhood were caught up in a whirl of social engagements, vanishing into the maze of the might-have-been. He did not revolt against this state of affairs; he allowed himself to float pleasantly down the river of the years, letting it carry him where it willed, sometimes twirled about in a violent eddy, sometimes basking peacefully in the shallows. Thus there is no suggestion of strife or revolt in his serious work, which conforms to accepted patterns; there is no discord, no attempt to reconcile the opposing forces within

H*

himself; all is conventional, agreeable, and what he would have called "musical." Even in his light operas the spirit of criticism was gradually ousted, the voice of disquietude in the form of parody was stilled, and after the success of *The Mikado* his musical treatment became more elaborate and more formal; though fortunately his sense of fun and gift of melody remained with him as long as Gilbert was there to provoke them.

The pleasure he derived from luxury and smart society became in later years the mainstay of his existence; and though his conscience sometimes pricked him, he made no attempt to recover the lost ground. Early musical friends were easily forgotten in the dazzling circle of Marlborough House, and Grove, Macfarren and the rest shook their heads in vain. For years he had failed them by his addiction to comic opera, his desire to earn large royalties; now he was failing them by his addiction to social functions, his desire to earn the praise of royalty. Joseph Bennett, who wrote the libretto for *The Golden Legend*, had a very high opinion of Sullivan's abilities and could not help feeling annoyed over the musician's immersion in society and the life of the Turf, an annoyance that crept into his published criticisms of Sullivan's later work; and since Sullivan was conscious of his failure to live up to the expectations of his musical mentors, and therefore extremely touchy on the subject, the friendship between himself and Bennett gradually cooled.

It is more than probable that Mrs. Ronalds had a great deal to do with Sullivan's descent from the art world to the smart world. There are few women who would rather see the man they love among his peers than among peers, and Mrs. Ronalds was not one of them. The flattery of a nobleman was so much more pleasant than the cautious appraisal of a musician; and so we may be sure that Mrs. Ronalds encouraged Sullivan along the primrose path of dalliance with dukes and duchesses. His illness hastened the descent. He wished to enjoy the painless hours, and the older he grew the less enjoyment did he find in composition. Persistent bad health enfeebled his resistance to the distractions for which he craved, and just as morphia eased his physical pain so did gambling and dining-out and horse-racing help to disperse the cloud of apprehension that darkened his mind in solitude.

During the last years of his life Mrs. Ronalds was to be seen with him everywhere: at the theatre, at race-meetings, at big social functions, they were inseparable. She even attended the auditions which were held at the Savoy, when she would sit in a box, Sullivan in the pit, Carte in the gallery and Cellier in the orchestra, and the nervous singers had to remember that hers was the casting vote.

On the relatively rare occasions when they were apart, Sullivan wrote or wired to her two or three times a day. But in London they passed several hours daily in one another's company. He gave dinner-parties and musical evenings in her honour, and the guests would often include the Prince of Wales, the Duke of Edinburgh, Earl This and Viscount That. The serious entertainment was provided by Sims Reeves, Edward Lloyd, Charles Santley, Tosti, Albani, Patey, Trebelli and other famous singers who had appeared in Sullivan's works, the comic element by Arthur Roberts, Rutland Barrington, George and Weedon Grossmith, and such-like humorists. When these parties were held on Sunday evenings the strictest secrecy was observed for the sake of the Prince, whose conduct would have been impugned from every Nonconformist pulpit in the kingdom if it had got about that he was enjoying himself in a purely secular way on the Sabbath. Sometimes, as a special treat, the Duke of Edinburgh would favour the guests with a violin obligato, or Mrs. Ronalds would sing *The Lost Chord* and wring tears from the greater part of that cultivated company. The parties were not always musical, and the Nonconformist clergy would have perished in their pulpits from apoplexy if they could have seen the heir apparent and his friends sitting round a table well into the early hours, the atmosphere thick with

tobacco smoke and the fumes of alcohol, playing
poker for stakes that even Rothschild could hardly
have described as economical.

But giving and attending parties did not occupy
enough of the twenty-four hours, and when Sullivan
was not forced to work he frequently occupied his
spare moments with experiments.   For years he
tried to improve on the "J" nibs with which he
wrote his music, and kept up an energetic correspondence with the makers, suggesting larger or
smaller sizes, thicker or narrower points.   He
invented a blind that rolled up when a button was
pressed. He made drawings and models for a score
of things that never got beyond the initial stages.
One of his inventions was adopted by the Prince of
Wales, but apparently by no one else. This was an
arrangement whereby a runaway horse was allowed
to run away from its carriage. A lever was pulled,
the shafts were released from the harness, the
carriage came to a full stop, and the horse was free
to gallop to its heart's content. The device was to
be known as Sullivan's Safety Shafts, but nothing
came of it, either because gentlemen drivers did not
like to be thought incompetent in the management
of a horse or because coachmen did not wish to
look foolish in the event of their nervous lady
employers using the lever when the horse was
merely being frisky.

Except when deep in a piece of music that had to

be finished by a certain date, Sullivan even welcomed the distraction of visitors while he was composing, and many of his melodies came to him in
the noise and bustle of a social crush, when he would
pull out a notebook and commit them to paper. He
scored with great rapidity, smoking cigarette after
cigarette and chatting without effort to the visitor
of the moment.

"Why, it's like writing shorthand," said George
Grossmith after watching him for a moment in
silence.

"Yes, but it's much quicker," replied Sullivan.

To many people he gave the impression of being
an incorrigibly lazy man; and since he often left
the overtures of his comic operas to be concocted by
Alfred Cellier or Hamilton Clarke, there was some
foundation for this; but when he had to work
seriously he did not stint himself; he shut himself up
during the dark hours and slaved away until he
was mentally exhausted. When we consider that he
was constantly subject to an extremely painful disease, that he was a busy conductor as well as composer, that he lived in an endless turmoil of social
engagements, and that, whether at work or play,
he burned the candle at both ends, we cannot help
marvelling at the stream of iridescent numbers
that flowed from him and gave his age its only link
with Merrie England.

2

Having put into music all the emotions aroused
in him by the Diamond Jubilee of Queen Victoria,
and dimly conscious of the fact that patriotic sentiment was dependent upon personal comfort,
Sullivan returned to comic opera in the autumn of
'97. Comyns Carr brought a libretto which he had
written with Arthur Pinero; and though at first
Sullivan was pleased with it, on second thoughts
he decided that it was too verbose. But Pinero was a
famous dramatist who suffered from the curious
delusion that he wrote natural dialogue and who
had such a high opinion of his stilted phraseology
that he would not bate a syllable of it to please a
host of critics. It was unlucky for Sullivan that in
this instance he should have jumped out of the
Gilbertian frying-pan into the Pineronian fire, for
Pinero was the true successor of Gilbert both as
autocrat producer and as dictator playwright.

Sullivan informed his collaborators that the
musical construction of the piece left much to be
desired. "What we have written, we have written,"
was their reply. Sullivan took a villa at Roque-
brune near Monte Carlo and wrestled with Pinero's
syntax. Carr went to stay with him, and often
accompanied him to Monte Carlo, where his fights
with grammar were easily forgotten in his fever for

gambling. He could not endure to be watched while playing, Carr tells us, and "if he caught sight of me anywhere near his table his resentment was eloquent." Apparently Carr did not realise that his presence reminded Sullivan of what he was most anxious to forget.

Other friends besides Carr sometimes caught glimpses of Sullivan at the tables and were horrified by his frantic absorption in the game. Bending over the table, the light shining on his wrinkled perspiring forehead and blazing eyes, he stretched out a hand crammed with gold pieces, a hand so shaky that sometimes the coins fell on the wrong numbers; but the croupier always allowed him plenty of time while his trembling fingers pushed the coins into place. So completely did he surrender to the excitement of the game that he was prostrated with exhaustion after three hours of it and had forgotten all about his winnings or losings, expressing astonishment when he discovered that his pockets were empty.

"The bandits here have had seven hundred of the best out of me this evening," he once confided to G. R. Sims as he tottered from the room; "I've lost every note I brought with me."

"Never mind," replied Sims encouragingly, "there are plenty more notes where they came from."

This joke gained considerable currency in the

witty 'nineties, and twenty years later found its way into the author's autobiography.

Having expended more labour on *The Beauty Stone*, as the Carr-Pinero libretto was called, than he had ever given to Gilbert's pieces, Sullivan was repaid with a seven-weeks run in the late spring of '98. That autumn he conducted the Leeds Festival, with which he had been associated for twenty years, and at the conclusion of the last performance the chorus cheered him so enthusiastically that he broke down and ran to his room to hide his tears. When he had recovered he came out and shook hands with them all. Afterwards he was cheered by the band when he saw them off at the station, and at supper he was serenaded by about thirty members of the male chorus, who were rewarded with champagne and cigars. "Rather a trying day," he wrote in his diary. In spite of his bad health he was looking forward to conducting the Leeds Festival in 1901 and hoping to mark the occasion of his public retirement with "a worthy successor to *The Golden Legend*." Meanwhile the Savoy Theatre was kept open with revivals of the Gilbert and Sullivan operas, and to celebrate the twenty-first anniversary of its original production *The Sorcerer* re-appeared on November 17th, '98. Sullivan conducted, and at the fall of the curtain there were the usual calls for Gilbert and himself. They entered from different sides of the stage, bowed to the audience, did not speak to one another, left the theatre separately, and never saw one another again.

With the weakening of his constitution, caused by his kidney complaint, his habits of life and repeated doses of morphia, Sullivan became the prey of mental instability and physical listlessness. Only two years before the revival of *The Sorcerer* Sir George Grove had described his personal appearance: "He was thin, but I thought his face very much improved, and *very* nice to look at." In disposition, too, he was at that time the man his friends had always known—affectionate, simple, amiable, happy, lovable—whose delightful smile made him quite irresistible. But by the end of '98 the effects of prolonged ill-health and over-indulgence of the senses began to appear. He became peevish and irritable, quick to take offence, angry over trifles. If people did not wish to play cards with him, he felt insulted and was rude to them. His manner was moody and morose. The change in his nature was also noticeable in his face. The eyes were losing their lustre, the plump cheeks were shrinking, the healthy complexion was gone, deep lines ridged the skin, which began to take on the appearance of shrivelled yellow parchment. He was no longer capable of sustained effort. He wanted to compose another oratorio, but could not summon up the energy. He would write furiously for a while and then fling what he had written into the fire; he would change his mind fifty times in a day. Often, in making up his diary, he had to think for half-an-hour before he could remember what had happened twenty-four hours earlier. He would smoke a cigarette, throw it away half-finished and instantly light another. He would leave his flat to pay a call, alter his mind before he had gone a hundred yards, return to the flat, decide to go somewhere else, and probably end up by going nowhere.

Though he had agreed to collaborate with Basil Hood in a new comic opera to be called *Hassan*, he found it almost impossible to settle down to work, and excused himself on the ground that as Carte had just produced an opera with an oriental setting, *The Lucky Star*, it would be unwise to do another piece with an Eastern atmosphere. Hood promptly sketched out a fresh plot, but Sullivan could not muster up the enthusiasm to deal with it, and after a brief attack of influenza he left for the Riviera, where he spent several months in comparative idleness, driving from one place to another, dining here and there, learning to play golf, and losing a lot of money in the usual way. June came, and he went to Switzerland, where Basil Hood joined him. After many walks and talks they decided to carry on with *Hassan*, and throughout August '99 Sullivan was composing the music intermittently, though the old ease and vigour had vanished; he was dissatisfied with nearly every number that he wrote, and he fretted continually over trifles that normally he would not have noticed. In the hope that inspiration would come with change of scene, he returned to England and took a house at Wokingham, where he finished *The Rose of Persia*, as they had now decided to call *Hassan*, on November 18th.

His work on it had been interrupted for the first five days of November while he was struggling with a poem by Rudyard Kipling. The Boer War had just broken out and had inspired Mr. Kipling with a number of verses entitled *The Absent-Minded Beggar*. At the request of the *Daily Mail* Sullivan undertook the production of an appropriate tune. Over a year ago he had tried to set Kipling's *Recessional*, but it had proved too much for him and he had given it up. This was a more serious matter. The whole country was bitten with Boer-phobia and it was his plain duty to provide another *Onward Christian Soldiers*. The metre of Kipling's verses baffled him. "Gilbert has given me a teaser this time," he had been known to say, but Gilbert's most difficult song was child's play compared with *The Absent-Minded Beggar*. However, like Macbeth, he bent up "each corporal agent to this terrible feat," and produced a tune that had the desired effect of making money for the dependants of those Christian soldiers who marched onward to its strains.

Sullivan had a market-mind; he was easily affected by the public response to his works. He thought highly of *Ivanhoe* until he realised that the public thought less highly of it, after which he thought less highly of it himself. He had a poor opinion of *The Rose of Persia*, but it was produced at the Savoy Theatre on November 29th '99 and ran for over two hundred nights, after which he had a better opinion of it. Carte was delighted. At last it really looked as if he would not in future have to rely on revivals of the Gilbert and Sullivan operas. But he was to be disappointed. When in due time *The Rose of Persia* withered away, the Gilbert and Sullivan operas remained his chief source of income.

With *The Rose* running to good houses Sullivan's mind wandered, as usual in such circumstances, among loftier themes, and with the turn of the century he was meditating a new oratorio. But now his mind was only capable of wandering, and after several vain attempts he settled down to the more congenial pursuit of doing nothing. Social life in London attracted him as much as ever, and he planned a number of schemes for the future. For a while he toyed with a suggestion by D'Oyly Carte that he should become the owner of the Savoy Theatre. He promised to do a second opera with Basil Hood. He thought of buying a house at Camberley, where he had spent a part of his youth. He arranged to conduct a number of concerts. Early in

January 1900 he was nearly killed by falling between
the platform and the footboard of a train at Crystal
Palace, but he dismissed the incident light-heartedly
and plunged into another round of pleasure and a
further set of plans. February saw him at Monte
Carlo. Still he was unable to concentrate on anything, but mooched about, mostly alone, the victim
of so many intentions that he lacked aim. By May
he was in Paris, where he received a request from
the Dean and Chapter of St. Paul's Cathedral to
compose a Te Deum for a Peace Celebration Service at the end of the Boer War. He replied that he
would do what he could.

At home again he saw the Prince of Wales's
horse win the Derby. The Turf attracted him even
more than the tables, and some of his happiest days
were spent at Newmarket or Ascot. It is probable,
if regrettable, that he would rather have owned a
Derby winner than written *The Mikado*. A fairly
good judge of form, he once backed an outsider in
the St. Leger, having taken 1000 to 40, and won;
and three months before his death he spotted the
winner of the next year's Derby at a suburban
meeting.

The news that Lord Roberts had just occupied
Johannesburg convinced him that the war was
practically over, and he started on the Te Deum;
but he suddenly received a telegram asking him to
conduct a special performance of *The Mikado* at

the Opera Royal in Berlin. The performance was
to be given in aid of hospitals, and the Kaiser particularly wished that Sir Arthur should conduct it.
Now it so happened that, in view of his favourable
attitude towards President Kruger, the Kaiser was
extremely unpopular in England; but Sullivan was
a man to whom crowns and coronets made a more
direct appeal than kind hearts; it is conceivable
that he would have sacrificed his own head for the
sake of a crowned head; even exiled monarchs,
e.g. the Empress Eugénie, claimed his "respectful
devotion"; and when he made his will he did not
forget the members of the English Royal Family.
So in spite of the Kaiser's unfriendly behaviour
over the Boer War, Sullivan abandoned his Te
Deum and travelled to Berlin. The performance
was a great success; he was called and loudly
cheered after each act, and received a summons to
the royal presence at the final fall of the curtain.
Following the congratulations, Sullivan was thanked
by the Kaiser for doing him the honour of coming to
conduct.

"The honour is mine," said Sir Arthur promptly.

His Majesty then discussed several points connected with the opera and presented Sir Arthur
with a set of studs and sleeve-links displaying the
imperial monogram and crown set in diamonds
and sapphires. Monarchs have invariably shown a
partiality for studs and sleeve-links, which may be

taken as a hint that the recipient should always dress for dinner. The Kaiser then said that he should very much like to visit England, but was not quite sure whether he could fit it in with his plans.

"I hope very much you will, Sir," said Sullivan.

"Why?" asked the Kaiser.

"Because if your Majesty were to come to England now, you would receive a grander reception than ever your Majesty has had before."

His Majesty was visibly pleased, and Sir Arthur, obviously suffering from a rush of royalty to the head, continued:

"Your Majesty has no idea how popular you are in England. The English are not demonstrative as a rule, but they know their friends and know how to appreciate them, and they fully appreciate your Majesty's friendship."

The Kaiser smiled and Sir Arthur proceeded to cap the last statement:

"At this moment your Majesty and Lord Roberts are the two most popular men in England."

"Ah! Lord Roberts!" exclaimed Wilhelm II: "Yes, he has done splendidly. Too much cannot be said of his success. I congratulate him warmly."

His Majesty was exceedingly pleased by this assurance concerning the feelings of the British nation for his person, and in taking farewell he expressed the hope that he would soon see Sir Arthur again.

Normally Sullivan was an extremely discreet man, but on this occasion, as he admitted, he allowed his enthusiasm to run away with his discretion and gave a press representative a report of the above conversation, which was promptly telegraphed to England and published in most of the papers. It created a minor sensation, and the *Westminster Gazette*, mistaking the Kaiser's gift to Sir Arthur for "a very precious set of sapphire buttons," asked the question: "What would the Emperor say if he came to England and saw us wearing over five million Baden Powell buttons? Would he think that we didn't care a button for *him*?"

Though he was furious with the press, what particularly agitated Sullivan was the annoyance of the Prince of Wales, who was not too pleased to have it told, on the authority of England's leading composer, that the Emperor of Germany was more popular in England than the Prince of Wales. For the next few months Sullivan was cursing himself heartily for his stupidity. All his life he had been most careful, most cautious, most diplomatic, most discreet. But somehow the excitement of the moment, the cheers of the audience, the royal congratulations, the wreath of flowers given him by Count Hochberg and the Opera Company, the sense of being an ambassador, the desire to mitigate international misunderstandings, the pride of being consulted by Imperial Majesty, the sleeve-links —everything had conspired to put him off his guard. Perhaps the real cause of his tactless behaviour had lain in his physical condition. He was no longer in command of himself; his tongue was at the mercy of his temperature.

Having attended several race-meetings "to still his beating mind," he spent July at Shepperton, where he finished the Te Deum, which he did not live to hear. He was much depressed by the deaths of three friends in quick succession: Sir George Grove died in May, the Duke of Saxe-Coburg in July and Lord Russell of Killowen in August. Movement, change of scenery, change of occupation became imperative, and he went off to Switzerland with Hood's new libretto, *The Emerald Isle*, in his trunk. For a fortnight he tried hard to recapture some of the old fire that Gilbert alone had been able to feed, but it was uphill work; he seemed "very short of ideas," and thought most of what he did "paltry stuff." In the middle of September he got drenched to the skin on his way to see the Duchess of York and caught a severe chill, which went to his throat and deprived him of speech. He wondered whether he was dying, and with one of those sudden impulses to which he was prone left Switzerland at a moment's notice and arrived home on the 19th. Here, at the end of the month, he again tried to work, but his inspiration seemed to have dried up and he suddenly decided to visit Tunbridge Wells.

Though he managed to put the finishing touches to the first act of the new opera, the fortnight he spent at Tunbridge Wells was a period of gloom and terror. Again he was attacked by the disease that had tortured him for nearly thirty years, and the doctor found him writhing with pain and soaked in perspiration. An injection brought relief, but the attack left him physically weak and a prey to nervous fears. Sometimes he went out for a walk; often he sat at a table, making heroic efforts to conjure music from the darkening world of his imagination; mostly he brooded despondently on the decay of his powers, the loss of family and friends, the mutability of human life and the end of all things. He left Tunbridge Wells on a day of sunshine, writing in his diary: "I am sorry to leave on such a lovely day."

Back in London, he found that the ability to work had completely deserted him, though he looked forward to conducting the first performance of a revival of *Patience* at the Savoy on November 7th. Three days before the opening night, however, he realised that he would not be able to stand the strain, and when Gilbert and D'Oyly Carte were bowing to a wildly enthusiastic audience Sullivan was in bed. A day or two later, as a result of exposure while making a lake in the grounds of his country house, Gilbert was laid up with rheumatic fever; but the news of Sullivan's serious illness had softened him, and he wrote to say that, but for his own condition, he would have called to see his old partner before going abroad for a cure. This letter of conciliation pleased Sullivan, who would have liked a farewell handshake with the man who had shared his greatest triumphs.

As the dreary November days crept onwards it became clear to his servants that Sullivan was dying. He had always been generous and considerate to his dependants and to his less fortunate fellow artists. Whenever he heard that some actor or singer of his acquaintance was in financial straits he used to send money, and there are stories of how he paid a fortnight's salary to one overworked girl at the Savoy in order that she might take a holiday, and the doctor's bill of another who had been ill for some time. Louis Jager, his valet, was especially fond of him, and could not restrain his tears when he realised that his master was dying.

"Why do you cry?" asked Sullivan one day. "I am perfectly happy and contented. You must not cry for me. How do you think I could be otherwise than happy when I am going to see my dear mother?"

On the evening of November 21st he appeared to be sleeping peacefully; but at six o'clock the following morning his nephew, housekeeper and valet were awakened by the loud ringing of his bell. They rushed into the room.

"My heart! My heart! " he cried.

His nephew moved him slightly to an easier position. At first he could only breathe with difficulty, and soon he could not breathe at all. The Royal Physician and Mrs. Ronalds, both of whom had been summoned by telephone, arrived too late to see him alive.

In August, 1882, Sullivan had written a number of directions for his burial, one of which was that he should be placed in the same grave with his father, mother and brother in Brompton Cemetery. But the wish of the Dean and Chapter of St. Paul's prevailed, and he was buried in the crypt of the Cathedral, the first part of the service being held, by the Queen's order, at the Chapel Royal.

Gilbert was ill in Egypt and did not hear of Sullivan's death till he read an account of the funeral. D'Oyly Carte, who only survived Sullivan by a few months, was also lying ill—so ill that the news of Sullivan's death was kept from him. His house in Adelphi Terrace overlooked the Thames Embankment, and some unaccountable instinct made him rise from his bed and drag himself to the window at the moment when the funeral procession was passing on its way to St. Paul's. A little later he was discovered lying exhausted on the floor.

"I have just seen the last of my old friend Sullivan," he said.

CHAPTER VI

GILBERT

I

"I HAD gout all my life till 1900," Gilbert told a friend, "when rheumatic arthritis came along. They eloped together—the only scandal I ever had in the family."

It was the latter disease that caused his absence from England when Sullivan died; it was the former that was partly responsible for the bitterness of his quarrel with Sullivan. All through the 'eighties and 'nineties he was a victim to gout, which imparted a virulence to his natural irascibility and involved him in a number of law suits. Like all quick-tempered men he bore no malice merely because of a quarrel, and would have echoed Prospero's words:

> they being penitent,
> The sole drift of my purpose doth extend
> Not a frown further.

Unfortunately the people who considered themselves grossly insulted were apt to feel impenitent, and Gilbert, backed by the gout, would not stop until he had publicly chastised them. His favourite work in literature was the Book of Job, in which he pictured himself as Jehovah when smiting his enemies, as Job when being smitten by them. No other English writer has appeared in the law courts as often as Gilbert, a full account of whose cases would fill a volume, which might also include a substantial index devoted to the proceedings he wished to institute and was painfully diverted from doing so. Most of his cases ended with a disagreement of the jury, or at least with little benefit to either side of the dispute, and Gilbert would complain of the judge's partiality or his counsel's incompetence. He described one judge as being in the last stages of senile decay and as having "summed up like a drunken monkey." Another time, in listening to his counsel's speech, he confessed himself charmed by the interest of the narrative as it was gradually developed, the only criticism that occurred to him being that the substance of the speech bore no relation whatever to the contention he had come into court to establish.

One case of his made a sensation because it brought him into open conflict with the press, the theatrical profession and. his fellow authors. In 1898 an actress named Miss Fortescue produced a new piece by him in the provinces. It was called *The Fortune Hunter*. Gilbert went to Edinburgh to see it and while there he gave an interview to the representative of a local paper, in which he railed against the critics, referred to Sydney Grundy as "a mere adapter," and said that poetic drama was dead because no English actor knew how to speak blank verse; he instanced the Shakespearean performances of Irving, Tree and Alexander, none of whom could make a poetic speech of thirty lines interesting to the audience and all of whom mouthed the verse like Eton and Harrow schoolboys on Speech Day. *The Era*, in commenting on this interview, said: "Mr. Gilbert's abnormal self-esteem has with advancing years developed into a malady. In his own estimation he is a kind of Grand Llama or Sacred Elephant of dramatic literature. The mildest criticism on his work, the most gentle disapproval of one of his plays, is a crime of lèse-majesté for which, if it were in his power, he would punish the culprit severely." *The Era* also spoke of "Gilbert the Great," of the succession of combats that had taken place to vindicate "the Gilbert Theory of the Universe," and of "the abnormal protuberance of his bump of self-esteem."

Gilbert promptly brought an action for libel against *The Era* and claimed a thousand pounds damages. Marshall Hall was among those who appeared for him, Edward Carson for *The Era*.

Marshall Hall, examining Gilbert, asked:

"You have read what was said in the article about your bump of self-esteem. Do you regard that as written in joke or seriously?"

"I can hardly take it seriously," replied Gilbert, "because I cannot suppose that anyone thinks I wish to reconstruct the universe. I am perfectly satisfied with Cosmos as it is." He added: "I have no theory of the universe and I am not a combative man"—a remark that was received with laughter in court.

The cross-examination was conducted by Edward Carson:

"You don't like reading hostile criticism?"

"I have a horror of reading criticism at all, either good or bad."

Pressed on the point, Gilbert admitted that he preferred reading unfavourable criticism: "I know how good I am, but I do *not* know how bad I am," he explained.

He was quite prepared to agree that *The Fortune Hunter* was a very bad play—"a play that fails is for all practical purposes a bad play," he said.

Carson then reminded him of what he had said about English actors in poetic drama and asked:

"Did you observe from the public press that a short time afterwards Sir Henry Irving, at a dinner of the Sheffield Press Club, spoke good-humouredly but warmly about the criticisms upon himself?"

"I do not admit that he spoke good-humouredly

but warmly," rejoined Gilbert. "I noticed that he spoke most angrily and most spitefully concerning me. He described me as a librettist who soared to write original comedy."

Asked what was the direction of current dramatic taste, Gilbert answered:

"In the direction of musical comedy; bad musical comedy, in which half a dozen irresponsible comedians are turned loose on the stage to do as they please."

"Will you mention one of them?"

"Oh, there are plenty of them!"

"I wish you would mention one."

"Well, take the pantomime at Drury Lane Theatre with the great Dan Leno." (Loud laughter.)

"But that only goes on a short time in the year."

"It goes on for a long time in the evening." (Laughter.)

"Do you really describe a pantomime as a bad musical comedy?"

"No, but I would describe a bad musical comedy as a pantomime." (Great laughter.)

"That is very clever," said Carson when the laughter had subsided. "But I would like to know what you mean by bad musical comedies. Give me the name of one."

"There are fifty of them."

"Give me one."

"I would say such a piece as *The Circus Girl*."

"Would you call it a bad musical comedy?"

"I would call it bad. I believe the manager calls it musical comedy." (Laughter.)

"Have they half a dozen irresponsible low comedians turned loose in *The Circus Girl?*"

"I do not know how many there are." (Laughter.)

Carson was not doing too well, and decided to change the subject. He tried to get an admission from Gilbert that a certain character in one of his plays was expressing his own sentiments concerning the critics.

"I do not hold myself responsible for all the sentiments expressed by all my characters," returned Gilbert.

Varying his line of attack, Carson wanted to know what complaint Gilbert had against the critics. Gilbert declared that there were fewer original plays on the stage because the critics drew no distinction between original work and translations or adaptations. As a boy he had translated the Greek dramatists, but had never considered himself the author of their works. "I have always given Sophocles the credit for his share of the work in them," he added amidst laughter.

Carson now tried another tack. Gilbert had quarrelled with a number of people? Gilbert refused to admit that he had. Was he not extremely touchy and quick-tempered? Certainly not. Well, had he not quarrelled with, for example, Clement Scott? Yes, he had written to Clement Scott nine years ago complaining of a criticism.

"You said: 'I am determined not to expose myself again to your insulting jibes'?"

"Yes, no doubt I wrote that."

"You were cool and calm?"

"Yes, calm and deliberate. I don't know my temperature at the time." (Prolonged laughter.)

Gilbert also admitted that he had brought a law-suit against Horace Sedger, who produced *The Mountebanks*, but denied that he had fallen out with him.

"You were friendly with him afterwards?" probed Carson.

"I was not friendly with him before," replied Gilbert.

Gilbert had scored off Carson all along the line, but Carson's turn came with his speech for the defendants, when he made it so hot for Gilbert that the latter, seething with retorts he was unable to utter, got up noisily and stamped out of court. After an absence of two and a half hours the jury could not reach an agreement.

It is stated in Lord Carson's authorised biography that Gilbert met Carson twice at dinner afterwards and cut him dead; and though authorised biographies are notoriously unreliable on every point where the vanity of their subjects is concerned, we

may accept this statement because it does not conflict with our knowledge of Gilbert.

After spending many hours of his early life in the
witness-box, Gilbert made up for it by spending
many hours of his later life on the Bench. In 1891
he bought Graeme's Dyke, a sham Tudor house
built in the 'seventies and situated in Harrow
Weald. The estate, which included a model farm,
covered a hundred and ten acres. A belt of trees
surrounded the house, from the grounds of which
there were extensive views of the county. Gilbert
turned the house into a museum, the grounds into
a menagerie. The house was soon crammed with
curios, the walls covered with photos, paintings
and sketches. The grounds were quickly overrun
with all sorts of animals, from Madagascan lemurs
to Brazilian monkeys. Gilbert altered the name of
the house, aptly some thought, to Grim's Dyke, for
he kept burglars and newspaper reporters at bay
with the help of spring guns. One of the former
managed to evade the guns, but failed to evade
Gilbert, who collared him and trussed him up for
the police. Whereupon one of the latter, anxious to
obtain an interview on the subject, also evaded the
guns and called at the house. The butler asked
Gilbert whether he would see the gentleman from
the press.

"Tell the man to go to hell!" roared Gilbert, his

voice echoing through the hall where the reporter was waiting.

The butler returned and delivered the message in a manner more in keeping with his station in life:

"Mr. Gilbert is extremely sorry but he wishes me to state that extreme pressure of work precludes him from the pleasure of seeing you this morning."

A fat female interviewer, though she gained access to him, would perhaps have preferred the explosion of a spring-gun. Hoping to put him in a good humour, she gushed over his dogs.

"Dear, sweet, delightful creatures!" she •cried; "it is wonderful how all dogs take to me at once."

"Not at all," remarked Gilbert: "it is not often that they get a bone to pick with so much meat upon it."

His reputation as a litigant was considerable, and when J. L. Toole called at his new home the comedian's first words on alighting from the carriage were:

"Here I am at last! I was afraid, if I put it off any longer, you'd bring an action against me."

However, Gilbert was about to exchange the rôle of plaintiff for that of magistrate. Not long after his appearance in the part of a country gentleman he was approached by the High Sheriff, who asked:

"You have, I believe, studied the law as a barrister and have a sound knowledge of it?"

"That is so," replied Gilbert, "but I hope you will not consider it an impediment."

In spite of his legal knowledge he was appointed a Justice of the Peace for the County of Middlesex, and in that capacity his moral fervour at last found an outlet. He seldom failed to appear on the Bench at the Edgware Petty Sessions, and culprits regarded him as an unholy terror. Cases of distress melted his heart and he was known to pay a poor man's debt to save him from prison; but cruelty to child or animal enraged him and the offender must sometimes have thanked his stars that there were legal limits beyond which the bitter old gentleman with the glaring eyes and cutting tongue could not go.

"You'll do that sentence, notwithstanding the Home Secretary," he once said, and such was the look on his face that the prisoner reconsidered his intention to appeal, feeling no doubt that, if he obtained a remission, existence in the neighbourhood of Edgware would henceforward be insecure.

Towards the close of his life Gilbert's name became a byword among motorists, who were subjected to the heaviest fines permissible by law for infringing the speed regulations. Indeed, many drivers used to take circuitous routes in order to avoid a neighbourhood where a temporary absence of mind, causing a rate of twenty-five miles an hour, might cost them ten pounds. One motorist, presuming on the fact that he belonged to a superior class of society and was therefore immune from laws that were laid down for the guidance of mere chauffeurs, was promptly chastened for his vanity while being punished through his purse. In fining him five pounds for reckless driving, Gilbert said: "Had you been a gentleman, I should have fined you ten."

In cases of attempted suicide Gilbert combined sternness with lenience. After binding over one such miserable offender to come up for judgment if called upon, he said: "If you attempt suicide again you will be brought before us and punished for both offences, but if you succeed you will be beyond our jurisdiction."

Gilbert took himself, if no one and nothing else, very seriously, and he was extremely sensitive about his position as a magistrate. A fellow clubman once sympathised with him for being unable to get his own way on the Bench, adding: "But after all it is not quite the same thing as the Savoy Theatre." Gilbert, stung to the quick, hotly resented the implication and insisted at some length that his judicial opinions were respected and followed.

"Once in three months I can get this same rise out of him; no one is so easy to draw," said the clubman to a friend directly Gilbert's back was turned.

Though, as we shall see, Gilbert could not leave the theatre entirely alone, he fell easily into the

I*

rôle of country gentleman and magistrate, abdicating his sovereignty in one realm for rulership in another. With his tall, upright, square-shouldered figure, his stiff and pompous gait, his fresh complexion, piercing blue eyes, mutton-chop whiskers, brusque manner and air of command, no one in his neighbourhood would have associated him with "first-nights" or footlights. His clothes and conversation were in keeping with his new character; he wore loud checks, horseshoe tie-pins, broad flappy "Jorrocks" coats, and his talk was of cattle and cucumbers.

Few men can have left such widely different impressions on their contemporaries as Gilbert did on his. Some people, especially women, thought him pleasant, simple, kindly, affectionate. Others, mostly men, found him overbearing, intolerant, conceited, offensive. The truth seems to be that he was instantaneously irritated by self-important folk, by those who thought a lot of themselves and gave themselves airs. There was no humbug about him; he hated anything in the nature of a pose; his manner was abrupt and direct; and he never went out of his way to make people feel comfortable. The consequence was that he was feared and hated by anyone whose vanity he had pricked, and as he saw a good deal of absurdity in everybody and everything, the only human beings who got on well with him were those who had no

exalted opinion of themselves. He had an essentially
critical mind; he believed in nothing. It would be
possible to prove from his works that he was a
socialist, a conservative, a cynic, a sentimentalist, a
monarchist, a republican, a reactionary, a revolu-
tionist. In fact, apart from his satirical genius and
business acumen, he was a typical easy-going,
unadaptable, independent, disrespectful, prejudiced,
grumbling Englishman, who scorned everything he
did not curse, accepted the conventions and made
fun of them. He was cantankerous in manner and
generous in deed. His sentimentality was screened
with bluster. While looking at the face of a friend
who had just died, he burst into tears, rushed from
the room, pounded down the stairs to the accom-
paniment of loud oaths, seized the butler and
bellowed wrathfully: "George, have you seen my
bloody umbrella?"

There was something a little grim beneath the
vivacity of his conversational manner. The settled
gravity of his countenance was almost menacing in
the sense of slumbering hostility it conveyed. His
wit, which came like quick lightning from a lower-
ing sky, usually consisted of a play on words, and
seldom achieved the flights of such a master as
Sydney Smith, wherein truth was epigrammatic-
ally revealed by humorous and imaginative apprehension. But Gilbert's facility in his particular
medium was unique and gained him a reputation

for acidity that made people nervous in his presence. He snapped his jokes, usually prefacing them with a little grunt, which, owing to a paucity of onomato-pœic signs, can only be rendered as "Hm." Two stories about him are so famous that they have gone into the language and must therefore go into his biography.

Standing in the entrance hall of the Haymarket Theatre after a performance, he was mistaken for an attendant by a man whose appearance did not appeal to him. Said the man:

"Call me a cab."

"Hm. Certainly," replied Gilbert; "you're a four-wheeler."

"How dare you! What d'you mean?"

"Well, you asked me to call you a cab, and—hm— I couldn't call you 'hansom'."

Chatting with a friend one day on the steps of his club, Gilbert was accosted by a stranger, who said:

"I beg your pardon, sir, but do you happen to know a member of this club, with one eye, called Mathews?"

"I can't say I do," answered Gilbert, adding after a grunt, "What's his other eye called?"

Equally characteristic of him, though not so well known, was his remark on hearing the story of the old trombone player who shut up a fly in his music-book and next night, when he came to the smudge, ran down the scale, explaining afterwards: "I don't know vot dat big note vos, but I blayed it."

"Are you sure it was a fly?" asked Gilbert. "It might have been a bee flat."

He had not, as we have seen, a high opinion of actors whose affectations laid them open to his rebuffs. A well-known amateur named H. Such Granville once accosted him in the foyer of a theatre: "Excuse me for speaking to you without an introduction, Mr. Gilbert. You may have heard of me. My name is Such, but I act as Granville."

"Oh, do you?" came the curt rejoinder. "Then I wish your name was Granville and you acted as such."

Of an actor who had made a great success in light comedy and who was notorious at the Garrick Club for his boisterous laughter and extravagant manner, Gilbert said: "He is not quite a gentleman, and he knows it, and he tries to laugh it off."

Gilbert wrote dozens of limericks, many of them unprintable, and was never at a loss for last lines when other limerick enthusiasts appealed for assistance. The Savoy company used to fill two steam-launches when they went up-river for summer picnic parties. Sullivan, if he accompanied them, would be in one launch, Gilbert in the other. On one such occasion Sullivan shouted across the water:

"I say, Gilbert, we are composing limericks and want your help; we have got as far as this—

> That sailor who stands at the tiller
> Is in love with a girl called Priscilla;
>   But she never was taught
>   To know starboard from port—

and now we are stuck for a last line. Can you give us one?"

"I think your best plan is to kill her," promptly obliged Gilbert.

The limerick craze was sometimes a nuisance, and at a party where everybody was engaged in this depressing pursuit he wrote a verse that started a new fashion:

> There was a young man of Tralee,
> Who was horribly stung by a wasp.
>   When they said "Does it buzz?"
>   He replied "Yes, it hurts,
> It's a horrible brute of a hornet."

One of the symptoms of excessive vitality in a man is his impatience with popular idols, especially those of his own generation. Gilbert was an iconoclast. He could not endure the praise that was lavished on men whose mental equipment was inferior to his. Several notabilities of his age, Gladstone and the German Emperor among them, were treated with derision in his works, and he had a much lower opinion of the eminent Victorians than any of the so-called iconoclasts of to-day have dared to express. His general view of certain contemporaries was roughly put in *Thespis*:

> Well, well, it's the way of the world,
> And will be through all its futurity;
> Though noodles are baroned and earled,
> There's nothing for clever obscurity!

He had the same pet aversions as Mr. Bernard Shaw, and for the same reason: Shakespeare and Sir Henry Irving. The first was the god of the critics' idolatry, the second of the playgoers'. He wrote a skit of *Hamlet* entitled *Rosencrantz and Guildenstern*, in which he arrived at the conclusion that

> Hamlet is idiotically sane
> With lucid intervals of lunacy.

He informed Mary Anderson that she would get full houses for the first few weeks of her production of *A Winter's Tale* (which he did not think "a well-constructed piece"), because the public were too lazy to read the play and would go to see it—once! He told a friend that he thought Shakespeare a very obscure writer. "What do you think of this passage?" he asked. " 'I would as lief be thrust through a quicket hedge as cry Pooh to a callow

throstle'." "That is perfectly plain," the friend
replied. "A great lover of feathered songsters,
rather than disturb the little warbler, would prefer
to go through a thorny hedge. But I can't for
the moment recall the passage. Where does it
occur?"

"I have just invented it," said Gilbert, "and
jolly good Shakespeare, too."

The curious thing is that he really did believe it
was "jolly good Shakespeare," and he never tired
of girding at the poet whenever he could seize an
opportunity.

"If you promise me faithfully not to mention this
to a single person, not even to your dearest friend,"
he confided to George Grossmith, "I don't think
Shakespeare rollicking."

But it was difficult to feel more than irritated with
a man who had been dead for nearly three hundred
years. Irving, on the other hand, was very much
alive—an Old Man of the Sea on the shoulders of
modern playwrights, an actor who thought himself
superior to any dramatist, who ordered a play as
another person might order a glove, to be dis-
carded if it did not fit him. Gilbert really hated
Irving and all he stood for: the apotheosis of the
actor at the expense of the author. And so, when a
lady asked him whether he had been to see Irving
in *Faust* at the Lyceum, he compressed the accumu-
lated anger of years in a single phrase:

"Madam, I go to the pantomime only at Christmas."

The success of another well-known actor, Beerbohm Tree, annoyed him because he had a very poor opinion of Tree's histrionic ability and disliked the way in which he was copying Irving's methods in the production of Shakespeare and cheap melodramas with effective parts for himself. Nevertheless, he could not help liking Tree as a man, and sometimes dropped in for a chat after witnessing one of his performances. Whether Tree appreciated these friendly visits or not is open to question. Once Gilbert went to see him as Falstaff, a performance chiefly notable because of the difficulties that had to be surmounted by a very thin actor when playing a very fat part. On this occasion Tree made special exertions to please Gilbert and was still perspiring freely when the latter appeared:

"Well, what do you think of my acting?" was the eager enquiry.

"I think the pores of your skin act remarkably well," Gilbert assured him.

Again, after his appearance as Hamlet, Tree, anxious for sympathetic appreciation, received this from Gilbert:

"My dear fellow, I never saw anything so funny in my life, and yet it was not in the least vulgar."

Which is the correct version of the oft-repeated "funny without being vulgar" story.

Many years later Tree was asked to take several plays to Berlin, and Gilbert remarked that the actor had been invited there by the Kaiser "with the malignant motive of showing the Germans what impostors we all are."

One of Tree's leading ladies, who appeared as the boy Lucius in *Julius Cæsar*, inspired Gilbert with a conundrum:

"Why is Miss —— like a bad photograph?"

The answer was: "Because she is under-developed and over-exposed."

Yet another actor who had a high opinion of himself did not escape the dramatist's unfavourable notice; and when it was announced that Arthur Bourchier was going to play Hamlet, Gilbert declared:

"At last we can settle whether Bacon or Shakespeare wrote the plays. Have both the coffins opened and whichever has turned in his grave is the author."

Except for Pinero, he did not think much of his fellow dramatists. At a supper party shortly before the production of a play by Henry Arthur Jones, someone asked him:

"What do you think of Jones's new title?"

"Don't know what it is," growled Gilbert.

"It's quaint, to say the least; he's going to call his piece *The Princess's Nose*."

"Hm," grunted Gilbert; "hope it'll run."

Late in life Gilbert suffered remorse for having said so many cutting things, and even tried to convince mere acquaintances that most of them had been imagined by his enemies with the object of discrediting him.

"I did meet Gilbert once or perhaps twice shortly before his death," Mr. Bernard Shaw informed the present writer. "He was quite friendly, but all I remember of our conversation is that he complained of the way people invented ill-natured witticisms and attributed them to him. He instanced the famous description of Tree's Hamlet as 'funny without being vulgar,' which Tree invented himself and then fathered on Gilbert."

We can appreciate the kindly intentions of an old gentleman who is anxious to be remembered as the gentle-hearted victim of other people's malignancy, but truth compels us to overlook his general disclaimer. Apart from the evidence of disinterested onlookers, we have the evidence of the law courts. With regard to his remark about Tree's Hamlet, a Quaker singer named David Bispham was present when it was made and has published the true version, as given above, in his *Recollections*. But even if we were unprovided with outside proof, it is in the highest degree improbable that an actor who fancied himself as Hamlet would invent and give currency to a saying which ridiculed his art at its most sensitive point. Actors, like other people, have their vanity.

2

At the beginning of his life Gilbert had wanted to take part in the Crimean War, and ever since his failure to see it as a soldier he had pictured the Crimea as a land of romance. The subject constantly cropped up in his conversation, and one unfortunate lady was forced to listen to his views on that famous campaign during the greater part of a dinner. She was no longer young and tried to make up for the deficiency by the liberal use of rouge and lip salve, which may have occasioned Gilbert's persistence with his historical theme. At last she could stand it no longer:

"But I don't remember the Crimean War," she protested.

"Don't you?" said Gilbert; "I am sure you could if you tried."

When at last he went to the Crimea in the late 'nineties he was on familiar ground and felt as if he were revisiting it after a long absence. The weather was fortunate; for though they were "chivying a wet day all round the Mediterranean," they did not catch it up until they reached Algiers on the return journey. He was enraptured by the Crimea, decided to return there at the earliest opportunity, and even commenced to write a book about it, the only work he ever did for love, since he had never written love verses nor verse of any kind for which he had not been well paid.

Most of the sight-seeing he did in later life was determined by rheumatism and the gout. As early as '93 he had to produce *Utopia Limited* on crutches, and reported the fact that he was unable "to do anything but swear for the last eighteen days." A few years later he was attending certain rehearsals in a wheel-chair, from which he issued instructions to the players. Then came rheumatism in such a virulent form that his weight was reduced by sixty pounds in about six days and his legs and arms were "of the consistency of cotton-wool." He went to Egypt, where it rained so hard that he thought of "starting for Margate, which is drier, cheaper and more bracing." The sulphur baths, which smelt like rotten eggs, did him no good, and the doctor told him that he would probably be a cripple for life. What chiefly annoyed him was that he was too feeble to wash the back of his neck.

While in Egypt, early in 1901, his health was not improved by a railway accident. His wife and Miss Nancy McIntosh, who lived with them, participated in the adventure. They left Cairo for a day's excursion by train, and were seated in a Pullman, when a tremendous bump shot them half down the carriage on to their faces. A further series of shocks bounced them about from side to side of the coach, and then they were left in a condition of disordered tranquillity. The engine had jumped the rails, plunged down an embankment and proceeded to belch forth volumes of steam. Their carriage came to rest close to the engine, and as Gilbert could not rise, owing to the weakness of his knees, there was for a time some likelihood that he would be braised alive. However, Miss McIntosh rose to the occasion, got him out, retrieved his hat, and walked over two miles under a severe sun to obtain transport of a safer if slower type. Seven people were killed and about twenty injured, so the Gilberts were lucky to escape with their grazes and bruises.

A diet of fish, vegetables and fruit did what doctors, sulphur baths and baking suns had failed to do, and Gilbert's health improved so rapidly in the first years of the century that he was soon in a condition to ask a friend: "What ought a married man of sixty-five to do who passionately loves a young widow whom he took down to dinner last night? God help him, as his peace of mind is shattered." His attitude to the medical profession, as a result of personal experience, had now become clarified:

"What's your boy going to be?" he asked Mrs. Alec Tweedie.

"He's going into medicine."

"Hm. I don't mind his going into medicine as long as his medicine doesn't go into me."

By 1902 gout and rheumatism were about to "elope together," and Gilbert bought an American locomobile, a steam car. Up to then he had jogged along comfortably behind his horses, which he called Bryant and May because they were "a perfect match," but with the car came trouble. He began by running into a parson on a bicycle. The parson was damaged, Gilbert took a somersault over the dashboard and landed on his head, and his wife was lodged nicely in a hedge "where she looked like a large and quite unaccountable bird's nest." Some weeks later they were, according to Gilbert, not exceeding two miles an hour (as a magistrate he might have doubted his evidence as a driver), when two ladies came by in a carriage; the horse shied, made for the nearest bank, upset the groom and one of the ladies, who was run over, and bolted with the other. The carriage was stopped; no serious damage was done; and both ladies agreed that it was the horse's fault. After that Gilbert knocked down a man who was so drunk that he apologised for getting in the way. At that time great hostility to motor cars was displayed by a large section of the community, and someone wrote to *The Times* suggesting that residents on country roads should retaliate on motorists with a rifle. The humour of this appealed to Gilbert, who went one better. He favoured the erection of sign-posts at certain strategical points along the road, carrying the words: "Motor shooting for a single gun." Eventually the steam car disappeared and he bought a Rolls Royce. Though he could not resist writing to the makers: "Your car Rolls but it won't Royce," he was quite satisfied with it.

Gilbert was devoted to Grim's Dyke, and seldom left it during the last ten years of his life, though we hear of him in Switzerland and Italy in the autumn of 1905, when he had the mortification of engaging apartments at a certain hotel and finding on arrival that the rooms were mysteriously occupied. Having relieved himself in language that did justice to his feelings, he went to another hotel, where he discovered that the part-owner of the place he had just abused was a famous radical M.P., whose hostility he had provoked on a previous occasion and who was revenging himself in the manner aforesaid. Gilbert could not at the moment recall how he had inspired the man's animosity, but upon reflection it occurred to him that he had introduced the M.P. to the woman who was now his wife. That explained everything and Gilbert frankly admitted that he had done the fellow "an irreparable injury." Another holiday was spent in Constantinople, where everybody was becoming interested in politics. "I have been strongly advised

to ally myself with the Young Turkish party,"
wrote Gilbert, "but unfortunately I was not furnished with her address."

Women were his main interest in life; and if we
accept the statement of one of them that he preferred women with brains, we are driven to con-
clude that he was extremely fortunate in finding so
much brain among so many beauties. The fact
remains that no guest at Grim's Dyke, after a
casual glance round the table, would have been
able to swear that Gilbert had a passion for feminine highbrows; the guest might indeed have been
forgiven for wondering whether he was dining with
a beauty chorus. Gilbert surrounded himself with a
bevy of lovely women, among whom there was
usually a reigning favourite, and he had a special
room in his house which he called "The Flir-
torium." At dinner a woman always sat on each
side of him; the men were never permitted to dally
over their port in the dining-room before joining
the ladies; and at fancy dress functions he antici-
pated a later fashion by appearing as an Arab
sheikh.

Though fond of dancing he perceived its main
disadvantage: "Every boy with an eyebrow on the
upper lip takes the *pas* of me here," he dolefully
confessed. Sometimes he would complain of his
age. "There was a time when I used to express
myself distinctly," he told a female friend, "but I

am rapidly relapsing into a condition of babbling dotage. I am a crumbling ruin—a magnificent ruin, no doubt, but still a ruin—and, like all ruins, I look best by moonlight." But when he was feeling up to the mark he would explain that he was the most beautiful person in the world, that his forty-eight inch waist was exactly right for a man in his sixties, that his weight was that of Apollo (not in marble), that his life had been faultless as clear crystal, and that he was the greatest genius of his age. Occasionally he would hint darkly at a Juanesque aspect of his character which existed only in his imagination. "One feels *so* safe and (involuntarily) good," he said in explanation of the fact that at the age of sixty-six there was not "the remotest chance of one's being a snake on another man's hearth." He advised a friend that, if ever she went into someone else's bedroom in a hotel, she should "be quite sure it's the bedroom you want. I always do." Asked whether he had recently seen much of a certain actress, he replied: "Not much; only her face and hands." And when invited to attend a concert in aid of the Soldiers' Daughters' Home, he regretted that he could not be present, but said that he would be delighted to see one of the soldiers' daughters home after the entertainment.

Such was his liking for pretty women that he would even risk a cold or a bilious attack for the sake of doing what pleased them. He once caught a bad chill from sitting on a damp lawn with "distinctly the loveliest copper-haired lady I have ever met," though after-reflection made him wonder whether he had caught it from eating a melon. "What will you have?" he asked another attractive woman at supper. "Whatever you have, I shall have; then I shall know exactly how you are feeling in the morning."

He could be rude, as we have seen, to women who adopted artificial methods of rejuvenation. "I fell on the back of my head and was only saved from concussion by my thick hair," said one of them. "Now you will never grudge that last five pounds you paid for it," rejoined Gilbert. Fussy women also got on his nerves. "Oh, do take care! There's a wasp on your sleeve! It'll sting you!" was the agitated warning he once received. "I have no great opinion of the intellect of the insect," came the dry reply, "but it is not such a fool as to take me for a flower." Nor did he care for the New Woman, and when he read that certain Suffragettes had chained themselves to the railings in Downing Street and shouted "Votes for Women," he remarked "I shall follow suit. I shall chain myself to the railings outside Queen Charlotte's Maternity Hospital and yell 'Beds for Men'." He was however the child of an age that remained in long clothes, and his conversation with women was always most proper. Describing an Elizabethan dress to a girl, he said: "The triangular thing in front is, I believe, called a stomacher—you will forgive me if I am wrong." Which was an excellent specimen of clean fun. His sense of propriety was extended to the stage, and though he was often more amusing he was never more Gilbertian than in giving evidence before a Joint Committee of Lords and Commons on the Censorship of Plays:

"If a strongly expressed love scene took place between a man and a woman sitting apart," said he, "that might be nothing; but if they were sitting together on a sofa with their arms round each other's waist and the dialogue was punctuated with kisses, the effect might be very undesirable."

This opinion was impressed on C. H. Workman, who played Jack Point in a revival of *The Yeomen of the Guard*. Gilbert complained that the actor was caressing Elsie and Phoebe with unnecessary warmth.

"Ah, yes, I see," returned Workman, "you would not kiss them more than once."

"Oh, indeed I would!" exclaimed Gilbert, "but I must ask *you* not to."

His interest in the stage never relaxed. He built the Garrick Theatre for John Hare and promised to build a theatre for Cyril Maude, but could not find a convenient site. While the foundations of the Garrick Theatre were being laid, a subterra-

nean stream was tapped and the water rose with
alarming rapidity. The danger over, Gilbert was
much relieved. "It certainly seemed most disastrous," he said, "and for some time I was in grave
doubt whether to continue building or let the
fishing." No longer an active playwright, he took
both pleasure and pains in training young and
lovely actresses to live up to their looks. Lily
Hanbury, Julia Neilson and Ellaline Terriss were
among his "finds," and they all received their early
coaching from him. Occasionally a pretty protégée
thought him a little too exigent in his demands for
her companionship or gratitude and kicked over
the traces. After teaching one girl and getting her
a part in a play at five pounds a week, he discovered
that she was "an ungrateful little cat" who considered everything he had done for her "as in the
natural order of things."

Although he had recovered his health by 1903,
Gilbert had lost his grip of the theatre. Five years
earlier he had issued an edition of the *Bab Ballads*,
and feeling that the original drawings were too
grotesque, he had toned the poems down by sub-
stituting a number of less extravagant illustrations.
That was the beginning of the end. It showed
that he had already become a respectable old
gentleman, frightened by the brutal force of the
young man whose soul looked through those early
sketches and whose desire to climb to the top of the

ladder was revealed in the caricatures of a malignant imagination. Thus it was only to be expected
that, in a period of calm caused by a recovery of
health at the age of sixty-seven, Gilbert should have
returned to his fairies; and in the spring of 1904
Arthur Bourchier produced *The Fairy's Dilemma* at
the Garrick Theatre. The rehearsals seem to have
passed off without friction and the play had a
friendly reception. Mr. Max Beerbohm's remarks
in *The Saturday Review* explain its failure: "Yes,
assuredly the whole play should have been written
in verse. Even so, however, it would not have
quite 'come off.' Verse is not the only thing that
it ought to have been written in; it ought also to
have been written in the 'seventies." The author
could not quite agree with his critic. People would
have appreciated the play's intention, Gilbert
declared, if it had been produced in the 'sixties. As
he had lived through the 'sixties he ought to have
known, and so we may judge the dramatic taste of
that period by a quotation from *The Fairy's Dilemma*.
The demon Alcohol is speaking:

A thousand pardons! Driving here from town,
My brand-new Demon motor-car broke down;
A puncture long delayed me. This fatality
Affects one's character for puncture-ality.

Mrs. D'Oyly Carte began to revive several of the
Gilbert and Sullivan operas in 1906, and though
Gilbert thought them badly done their success was

enormous, and people realised for the first time that they were classics, independent of their period. The revival of *The Mikado*, which Mrs. Carte projected, was forbidden because the Japanese, then the allies of Great Britain, asked for its suppression—"a delicate and polite action on the part of a guest towards a host," Gilbert called it, comforting himself at the same time with the feeling that in three years England would be at war with Japan over India, when he would be offered a high price to permit its performance.

In 1909 Gilbert's last opera was produced at the Savoy Theatre. It was suitably entitled *Fallen Fairies*. Like the famous lozenge plot, the idea for this opera had been floating about in his mind for a long time. In fact the libretto was taken holus-bolus from a blank-verse play of his called *The Wicked World*, produced in the early 'seventies and described by a critic as "coarse" and "foul" because one of the characters said: "I go to that good world where women are not devils till they die." Gilbert had of course brought an action for damages, and after deciding that both play and criticism were entirely free from offence, the jury (obviously composed of Gilbertians) had returned a verdict for the defendants.

The story had been turned down by Sullivan and by Carte because there was no male chorus; it had then been offered to Elgar, who rejected it with-

T—g

out comment, to Messager, Massenet, Liza Lehmann and A. C. Mackenzie, all of whom disliked it
because of the absence of a male chorus.   But
Gilbert was never satisfied until he had squeezed
every penny of profit from a plot, and at length his
obstinacy was rewarded.   Edward German agreed
to do the music.   Gilbert was now in his element.
He had full control of the production down to the
minutest detail, and not only insisted that there
should be no tenor in the cast, but again tasted the
joy of teaching every member of the company how
to speak blank verse and rehearsing every piece of
"business," every movement, modulation and gesture, until he had achieved the effect at which he
aimed.   Above all, he had the unspeakable pleasure
of engaging the female chorus.   German had a word
to say as to their voices, but Gilbert was the sole
arbiter of their faces and figures, and since he
wished to be solely responsible for their training he
recruited them mostly from the Royal College of
Music, the Royal Academy of Music and the Guild-
hall School of Music.   Had he lived in the days of
Equity, his beauty chorus would have been more
expensive and more experienced.

Although seventy-three years of age, he had quite
enough energy to cope with his troupe of beginners,
over whom he tyrannised with patriarchal solici-
tude.   Indeed, according to Joseph Harker, he seems
to have had energy to spare.   Harker was engaged

to paint the scenery for the production. A generation earlier he had helped his uncle with the
scenery for *The Wicked World* and Gilbert had
approved his plan of basing the scenes for the
present production on those that had done service
for the original play. When Harker had nearly
completed the work Gilbert called to inspect it.
At first Harker was quite disarmed by the warmth
of Gilbert's greeting, and wondered whether old
age had transformed the lion into a lamb. He was
not kept long in a state of wonderment. The moment Gilbert cast his eye over the finished scenes
he demanded drastic alterations. Harker said that
it was too late to do anything about it now; Gilbert
had approved the original plan, and if he wanted
something different he must pay for the new
scenes and postpone the production. Instantly the
lamb disappeared, the lion reasserted itself, and for
ten minutes Harker listened to a roar of rage: "I
have seldom heard more violent abuse hurled by
anyone than that with which Gilbert assailed me
on this occasion." The roar having spent itself,
giving way to a succession of forest murmurs,
Harker's turn came. He informed Gilbert that
such behaviour was out-of-date and not to be tolerated, and that though he was aware of Gilbert's
habit of bullying those who could not afford to
answer him back, he (Harker) was independent of
Gilbert's patronage and would stand no nonsense

K

from him.   Gilbert gasped, growled, glared, and with a quick change of animal spirits left the studio trumpeting like an elephant.

At the fall of the curtain on the final dress-rehearsal Gilbert made his usual little speech to the performers and staff: "Principals, Director, Orchestra, Managers and Chorus, if the play succeeds, the credit is yours; if it fails, the fault is ours." But he also made a little speech to the audience, in which he said that he had received the whole-hearted assistance of everyone concerned with the solitary exception of the scene painter, who had opposed him on several vital points.

Had *Fallen Fairies* been successful, Gilbert intended to collaborate with Edward German in an opera based on another early play, *The Palace of Truth*; but it was a failure, and he decided never to write another libretto. In view of his public assertion that, if any, he preferred to read unfavourable criticisms of his works, it should be recorded that his wife was careful to show him only those notices which she considered were not likely to upset him, i.e. favourable ones. He hated having his actions, sayings or works subjected to the cool comment of people who could not feel as he felt; and once, on leaving the law courts, he would not even buy a paper when the placards in the Strand bore the words: "Gilbert's caustic remarks in the witness box." To the end of his life he remained ultra sensitive, not only to criticism, but to any act which might conceivably be interpreted as hostile. For example, William Boosey, who had bought the rights of Offenbach's *Brigands*, for which Gilbert as a young man had written the libretto, wished to produce it in the days of the librettist's fame and wrote to Gilbert offering to pay him if he would revise it. Gilbert replied that his version of the opera was a hack translation for copyright purposes, never intended for performance on the stage, and said that he would "always retain a vivid sense of your discourtesy in not consulting me in connection with your proposal to revive the work." He then applied for an injunction to restrain Boosey from producing the piece, but it was not granted.

One of Gilbert's earliest plays was a dramatised version of Dickens's *Great Expectations*. His last work was a Dickensian essay in cockney horror describing the Fagin-like imaginings of a murderer under sentence of death, and though it has no particular value as an index to his mind it proves that he had a wonderful faculty for discovering latent talent. He went to see James Welch in a comic part and perceived a tragic actor beneath the buffoon. So, having spent an hour in the condemned cell at Pentonville in order to get the right atmosphere, he sat down and wrote his grim little sketch, with the result that in 1911 Welch appeared in *The*

Hooligan at the Coliseum and made a big hit in the piece. The curious thing is that the criminal dies before reaching the scaffold, and the verdict, "Dead—Heart Failure," which were the last words Gilbert wrote for the stage, was pronounced by the doctors on the author's death a month or two later.

Gilbert, at the close of his life, had a poor opinion of the works he had written. "I fancy," said he, "that posterity will know as little of me as I shall of posterity." Sometimes he gave way to the bitterness of a man who had completely failed in his main endeavour. "If it's a poor play, it's sure to succeed," he prophesied of Sarah Bernhardt's production of *Lysianne*; "no good play is ever a success; fine writing and high morals are hopeless on the stage. . . . I have been scribbling twaddle for thirty-five years to suit the public taste and ought to know . . . Light flippery and amusing nonsense is what I have endeavoured to write; but I can tell you that after thirty-five years of that sort of thing, which I'm glad to say has brought grist to the mill, I am about sick of it, and I shouldn't mind if I never wrote another word."

"But are you not very proud of having acquired all this out of your own brain?" asked a visitor to Grim's Dyke.

"Not at all," replied Gilbert; "it represents the folly of the British public."

He would have liked to have known that a dozen

libretti containing his "twaddle," his "light flippery and amusing nonsense," had outlasted all the solemn, sombre, earnest and purposeful works of the Victorian Age. The knowledge might have made him grunt with disapproval, but it would certainly have made him chuckle with glee.

3

Like most people who are not at ease with their contemporaries, Gilbert adored children and dogs. They did not contradict or criticise him; they looked up to him; while he could influence their actions and play the god in their little world. For a man who remembered and often referred to the slightest and most imaginary affront, the company of a small girl or a large dog was soothing, and so he was to be seen at his happiest when playing with either. But any form of helplessness, any appeal for advice or sympathy brought out the best in him. He loved to be consulted, to be depended upon, to champion the oppressed, to act the fairy godfather. In his productions he always looked after the interests of the chorus and the small-part people, defending them from managerial depredations. He was the honorary secretary of the Bushey Heath Cottage Hospital from its commencement till his death, and frequently gave financial assistance to its poorer patients after they had left.

He financed a young man who wished to volunteer for the South African War, but could not afford to do so. To many who had failed in life, or who lacked the means to make good, he was extremely generous. "When I feel at all, I feel strongly," he once said, and he gave practical effect to his feelings.

He had driven many hard bargains in his life, and very few people got the better of him in business. In offering to write a play for Mary Anderson, he asked for five thousand guineas to be paid on completion, the piece to be hers for five years; and few things irritated him so much as the pirating of his operas in America. He thought it a scandal that copyrights should ever expire: "they ought to be freehold, like land," he declared. Thus it is not surprising that, in spite of his generosity, he left nearly £111,000 at his death. Sullivan, being a gambler, left rather less than half that sum; Carte, being a different sort of gambler, left much more than double that sum.

Gilbert only gambled with words, and in that respect was quite reckless. Owing to his amazing faculty for rhyming and conjuring with phrases, a faculty which gave such colour, variety and vigour to the comedy in his operas, he came completely under their spell in later life, a victim to verbal inversion, a logomachist. He simply could not resist a pun or a play on words.

"Rather a nice little wood, that," remarked a visitor who was being taken round the estate at Harrow.

"It would if it could but it can't," replied Gilbert.

"Yes, she's quite nice," he said on another occasion, the subject of conversation being a certain plump dame, "only I prefer a woman to be as long as she is broad."

At the age of sixty-nine he walked to London and decided that, as sixty-nine turned upside down was ninety-six, he would probably live to the latter age if he survived the former. The conclusion, he admitted, was founded on the topsy-turvy method of reasoning for which he was famous. Upon being told that excessive activity was dangerous in a man of his age and that he was tempting Providence, his comment was: "If Providence can't resist *my* humble temptations, how can I be expected to resist His?"

It is to be feared that, in his last years, he would have been quite capable of returning a greeting of "Hullo!" with the statement "My hull is not low." But there were brighter moments.

Meeting a judge named Kekewich, who said that he liked all the Savoy operas except *Trial by Jury*, Gilbert remarked: "He seemed to think that in holding the proceedings up to ridicule I was trenching on his prerogative."

An evening paper having referred to him as "the late W. S. Gilbert," he drew the editor's attention

to the error: "There is a line in your issue of yesterday that must have sent a thrill of joy through
many a worthy home . . . I am always sorry to spoil
sport, but common candour compels me to admit
(reluctantly) that I am still alive."

"I propose calling an early chapter in my book
'The Nebulous Stage'," said his first biographer.

"Does that refer to you or to me?" he queried.

His neighbour at Harrow was Mr. Blackwell, of
the famous firm of jam manufacturers, on whose
estate two of Gilbert's men had trespassed in order
to retrieve some tame pheasants. Mr. Blackwell
wrote to complain that they had done a certain
amount of damage, which called forth this:

"Dear Mr. Blackwell.

"I am exceedingly sorry that my men should
have damaged your preserves.

"Yours very truly.

"W. S. GILBERT.

"Pardon the word 'preserves'."

He shared with many men a dislike of conversation while his hair was being cut, but if the hair-
dresser had been as sensitive as himself he might
once have had his throat cut as well.

"When are we to expect anything further, Mr.
Gilbert, from your fluent pen?" asked the barber.

"What do you mean, sir, by fluent pen?" demanded Gilbert angrily. "There is no such thing

as a fluent pen. A pen is an insensible object. And, at any rate, I don't presume to enquire into your private affairs; you will please observe the same reticence with regard to mine."

At the age of seventy, which he described as the prime of life, Gilbert was the guest at a dinner given in his honour by the O.P. Club. Many of the Old Savoyards were present, and Gilbert got the biggest laugh of the evening when in the course of his speech he plaintively confessed: "Everybody says I'm such a disagreeable man, and I can't think why!" There was something curiously naïf about Gilbert. Nothing made him so angry as when he was accused of short temper; and it never dawned on him that people could think him disagreeable merely because he liked to have his own way. Actually it would be untrue to call him a disagreeable man, but it would be equally untrue to call him an agreeable one. It was remarked at the O.P. Club dinner that his face wore a "fiendish expression" while the orchestra played the airs of Sullivan, because, some said, they were unaccompanied by his words. Such an assumption could be justified by a story of Durward Lely's:

"Very good, Lely, very good indeed," said Gilbert at a rehearsal; "but I have just come down from the back seat in the gallery, and there were one or two words which failed to reach me quite distinctly. Sullivan's music is, of course, very beautiful, and I heard every note without difficulty, but

K*

I think my words are not altogether without merit, and ought also to be heard without undue effort. Please pay particular attention to the consonants, the Ms, the Ns, and especially the Ss."

But it is possible that if the "fiendish expression" had appeared on another man's face in similar circumstances, he would have been given the credit of indigestion. Since Gilbert was Gilbert, he was given the discredit of jealousy. A man who is labelled is generally libelled.

In 1907, twenty-four years after Sullivan had been knighted, Gilbert received a title which he described as "a tin-pot, twopenny-halfpenny sort of distinction." His first impulse was to refuse it, since it would merely confer on him an honour already enjoyed by money-lenders, soap-sellers and political sycophants. "This indiscriminate flinging about of knighthoods is making me very nervous," he said; "it's quite possible they may give one to my butler. He's a very good fellow, and I'm afraid it will upset him." Upon consideration he made up his mind to accept it, because he would be the only dramatist who had ever received it for his plays alone, and it would confer some distinction on his profession. Accordingly he went through the ceremony of being tapped on both shoulders by King Edward VII. But he was very much put out by the discovery that he was described as a "playwright" on the official list, as if his work were in the same mechanical category as that of a wheelwright, a millwright, a wainwright or a shipwright. After all, one never spoke of a novelwright, a picture-wright, a poemwright, a symphonywright or a statuewright. Then why playwright? Why not dramatist? He felt insulted, and was reminded of the incident at Windsor when *The Gondoliers* was attributed solely to Sir Arthur Sullivan. A dinner to celebrate the addition of what he called "an unmeaning scrap of tinsel" was held at a moment when the Old Age Pensions Bill was before Parliament, and he took the opportunity of telling the world what he thought of his knighthood:

"I am disposed to regard it rather in the light of a commuted old age pension; and if I may venture to make a suggestion to the right honourable gentleman at the head of the Government, it is that a knighthood conferred upon all working-men of sixty-five years of age and upwards would afford a cheap, effective and highly picturesque solution of what promises to be a problem of no little financial difficulty."

The right honourable gentleman at the head of the Government did not think this a bit funny; but he ought to have known that Gilbert was incapable of taking a title seriously.

"What must I call you now?" asked a female friend: "Sir William?"

"Call me 'Bill,' " he said.

"Very well, I'll call you 'Sir Bill'."

"I will do the billing if you will do the cooing," came the characteristic retort.

He was far more pleased over the invitation he received from the committee of the Garrick Club to become a member than over the "mere triviality" of the title. Not a naturally clubbable man, he was fond of what are known as smoking-room stories. His strict propriety in writing put a severe strain on his normally high spirits, which found vent in numberless yarns of a strongly Rabelaisian flavour. For many years typescript copies of a supposedly Gilbertian play were stealthily shown and furtively read in certain circles; and though without positive evidence no careful biographer could assign it to Gilbert, there are two strong arguments in favour of his authorship: (1) that it is as witty as any of his libretti, and (2) that it does show the demoralising effect of writing about seventy plays in which there was not a line "that the sensitive modesty of a young girl might shrink from hearing."

But Gilbert's club conversation did not wholly consist of unprintable stories. He was keenly interested in crime and criminals, and was an authority on the famous murders of the past. Once he called on Anthony Hope to impress upon him that the murder of William Weare by Thurtell and Co. had taken place close to a house at Radlett which the novelist had rented for several months, and that the scene was re-enacted by the ghosts on a certain night every year close to the front gates. "Fortunately that particular night is outside the term of your tenancy," said Gilbert, "but of course they might make a mistake in the date." A more gruesome episode is recounted by Pett Ridge. One day towards the end of October, 1910, Gilbert entered the Garrick Club and said that he had spent the morning at the Old Bailey listening to the Crippen case. He was in a bad temper, criticised the food, cursed the wine and expressed contempt for the cigars. At four p.m. an Under-Sheriff arrived with the news that Crippen was to hang. Gilbert brightened up at once and frankly admitted that his irritation during lunch had sprung from the fear that Crippen might get off.

In addition to crime he was devoted to croquet, deriving much pleasure from putting a ball through the hoop, while another hobby was photography. His literary tastes were not catholic. He liked Dickens, disliked Kipling, liked Trollope, disliked Jane Austen. His social tastes were equally exclusive, and when two theatrical "stars" turned up unexpectedly they had to thank Gilbert's love of animals for their entertainment. "The horse must be fed," he told his wife, "so the man and woman can have some dinner."

His health had never been better than in the last year of his life; and though he told one female friend that "the old crumbling ruin has been propped up and under-pinned, and will, I think, stand for a few months yet," he was quite annoyed with another who said he ought not to walk from Harley Street to Eaton Square immediately after lunch. "Walk!" he cried; "of course I'll walk. I walk six or seven miles a day. I never wore a pair of glasses in my life and I still feel eighteen." He was always most carefully dressed when he came to London for a round of visits, and during the summer months was frequently to be seen in a white topper and a light grey suit. He never stayed in town without going to the theatre, though he seldom displayed much enthusiasm for the plays he witnessed.

"Well, what did you think of it?" asked Weedon Grossmith, who was appearing in a play called *Baby Mine* at the Criterion.

"The half that I've seen is all right," Gilbert replied; "but I must come again, sit in the box on the other side and see the other half. I suppose these boxes are intended to make you see a play twice."

There were, of course, occasional moods of depression, in one of which he wrote: "Men of my age are like trees in late autumn—their friends have died away as the leaves have fallen from the trees." But on the whole he was remarkably cheerful: "The country is looking lovely, and I myself am very pretty." And five days before his death he told Sydney Grundy: "My experience is that old age is the happiest time in a man's life. The worst of it is, there's so little of it."

The morning of May the 29th, 1911, was warm and sunny. Gilbert had arranged to bathe in his lake that afternoon with two pretty girls, Miss Ruby Preece and Miss Winifred Emery, but he went up to town early in order to see the Annual Parade at the Royal Hospital, Chelsea, of which an old friend of his was Lieut.-Governor. Then he went on to the Junior Carlton Club for lunch. W. H. Kendal, the actor, was lunching alone and was amazed when Gilbert walked up to his table and said:

"Kendal, can I lunch at your table?"

In view of the fact that they had not been on speaking terms for more years than he could remember, it was a strange request, but Kendal replied:

"You have been a member of this club for twenty years, and can lunch at any table you like. I believe that is one of the rules of the club."

Gilbert promptly sat down and began talking about old days, of Mrs. Kendal and her brother Tom Robertson, of old plays and dead players. He was full of spirits, ate an enormous meal, and, though he had quarrelled with both Kendal and his wife nearly a generation before and ignored them ever since, he praised them now in such extravagant terms that Kendal was too astonished to eat his lunch. The meal over, Gilbert went on talking for a while, then looked at his watch, got up, said: "I must be off, as I've an appointment to teach a young lady to swim," shook hands warmly and went away. Before leaving the club he returned twice to shake Kendal cordially by the hand.

He next visited Miss Fortescue, an actress who had appeared in many of his plays and who had been thrown from her horse in the Park and was lying in a darkened room, her optic nerves having been affected by the accident. After chatting with her for a time he left the room and had a word with her mother.

"I won't ask what you think of her appearance," said the mother, "for you can scarcely see her."

"Her appearance matters nothing," answered Gilbert; "it is her disappearance we could not stand."

He caught the three-twenty train from Maryle-bone, motored the two girls from Harrow station to Grim's Dyke, and since the day was hot, they wasted no time in preparing for their plunge. Both the girls were in the water before Gilbert appeared. Neither of them could swim well; neither was aware that the lake was eight feet deep in the centre; and so when Miss Preece found that she was out of her depth, she became frightened and called to her companion for assistance. At that moment Gilbert arrived at the steps, shouted "It's not very deep, don't splash, you'll be all right," dived in and swam rapidly towards her. "Put your hands on my shoulders and don't struggle," was his command the moment he reached her. She did so; but the strain had been too much for his weak heart, and when she grasped his shoulders he sank beneath her. She sank, too, but came to the surface in a moment, felt the mud beneath her feet and struggled to the bank. Of Gilbert there was no sign. They called to him frantically. A gardener came, unmoored the boat, and after an age, as it seemed to the girls, brought the body to land. Artificial respiration was tried; but Gilbert had died from syncope, not suffocation, exactly an hour after he had left London in good health and high spirits.

"I should like to die upon a summer day in my own garden," he once said.

His wish had been granted.

AUTHORITIES

Some Unpublished Correspondence.

The Gilbert and Sullivan Journal, 1926-35.

The Works of W. S. Gilbert.

The Dictionary of National Biography.

W. S. Gilbert: his Life and Letters, by Sidney Dark and Rowland Grey, 1923.

Sir Arthur Sullivan: his Life, Letters and Diaries, by Herbert Sullivan and Newman Flower, 1927.

W. S. Gilbert, by Edith A. Browne, 1907.

Sir Arthur Sullivan, by Arthur Lawrence, 1899.

Arthur Sullivan, by H. Saxe Wyndham, 1903.

Arthur Seymour Sullivan, by Henry Saxe Wyndham, 1926.

About Music, an Address by Sir Arthur Sullivan, 1888.

Gilbert and Sullivan, by A. H. Godwin, 1926.

Gilbert, Sullivan and D'Oyly Carte, by François Cellier and Cunningham Bridgeman, 2nd edn, 1927.

The Story of Gilbert and Sullivan, by Isaac Goldberg, 1929.

The Savoy Opera, by Percy Fitzgerald, 1894.

The Story of the Savoy Opera, by S. J. Adair Fitz-Gerald 1924.

Gilbert and Sullivan Jottings, by Shelford Walsh, 1913.

Operatics, by Shelford Walsh, 1903.

The Life and Letters of Sir George Grove, by Charles L. Graves, 1903.

The Eighteen-Eighties, edited by Walter De La Mare, 1930.

The Life and Reminiscences of Jessie Bond, as told by herself to Ethel Macgeorge, 1930.

Rutland Barrington, by Himself, 1908.

A Society Clown, by George Grossmith, 1888.

Piano and I, by George Grossmith, 1910.

A Book of Famous Wits, by Walter Jerrold, 1912.

Portraits of the Eighties, by Horace G. Hutchinson, 1920.

English Dramatists of To-day, by William Archer, 1882.

Reading, Writing and Remembering, by E. V. Lucas, 1932.

Recollections of a Savage, by Edwin A. Ward, 1923.

Pages from an Adventurous Life, by Dick Donovan.

Some Eminent Victorians, by J. Comyns Carr, 1908.

Coasting Bohemia, by J. Comyns Carr, 1914.

Studio and Stage, by Joseph Harker, 1924.

A Player Under Three Reigns, by Sir Johnston Forbes-Robertson, 1925.

Dame Madge Kendal, by Herself, 1933.

A Few Memories, by Mary Anderson, 1896.

Forty Years on the Stage, by J. H. Barnes, 1914.

Melodies and Memories, by Nellie Melba, 1925.

Impressions that Remained, by Ethel Smyth, vol. 2, 1919.

A Quaker Singer's Recollections, by David Bispham, 1920.

Fifty Years of a Londoner's Life, by H. G. Hibbert, 1916.

My Life, by George R. Sims, 1917.

Records and Reminiscences, by Sir Francis C. Burnand, vol. 2, 1904.

Musicians and Mummers, by Hermann Klein, 1925.

Thirty Years of Musical Life in London, by Hermann Klein, 1903.

A Story Teller, by W. Pett Ridge.

Me and Mine, by Mrs. Alec Tweedie, 1932.

My Table-Cloths, by Mrs. Alec Tweedie, 1916.

Empty Chairs, by Squire Bancroft, 1925.

A Playgoer's Memories, by H. G. Hibbert, 1920.

The Wheel of Life, by Clement Scott, 1897.

The Drama of Yesterday and To-day, by Clement Scott, vol. 2, 1899.

Old Days in Bohemian London, by Mrs. Clement Scott, 1919.

The Life of Lord Carson, by Edward Marjoribanks, vol. 1, 1932.

London Letters, by George W. Smalley, vol. 2, 1890.

Anglo-American Memories, second series, by George W. Smalley, 1912.

A Sporting and Dramatic Career, by A. E. T. Watson, 1918.

Jimmy Glover His Book, by James M. Glover, 1911.

My Lifetime, by John Hollingshead, 2 vols., 1895.

A Musician's Narrative, by Sir A. C. Mackenzie, 1927.

Memories and Notes, by Anthony Hope, 1927.

Past Times and Pastimes, by the Earl of Dunraven, 1922.

Memories of Half a Century, by R. C. Lehmann, 1908.

Personal Reminiscences of Sir Henry Irving, by Bram Stoker.

Ellen Terry's Memoirs, 1933.

Fifty Years of Music, by William Boosey, 1931.

Ellaline Terriss, by Herself, 1928.

A Chronicle of Friendship, by Luther Munday.

Studies in Literature, Third Series, by Sir Arthur Quiller-Couch, 1929.

The London and Provincial Daily Press, May 30 and 31, June 1, 1911.

The London and Provincial Daily Press, November 22-23, 1900.

The Theatre, April 2, 1883.

The Theatre, May-June, 1877.

The Era, April 2, 1898.

Cornhill Magazine, December, 1863.

Pall Mall Magazine, vol. 23, 1901.

Scribner's Monthly, vol. 18, 1879.

Strand Magazine, December, 1925, December, 1926, January, 1927.

Holly Leaves, 1880.

The Bookman, July, 1911.

McClure's Magazine, vol. 20, January, 1903.

Cassells Magazine, March, 1900.

The Literary Digest, New York, July 25, 1914.

The Critic, New York, September, 1901.

The Times Law Reports, 11.T.L.R.4., 1894.

The Times, August 21, August 28, September 4, 1890, September 29, 1931.

Daily Telegraph, March 29-30, 1898, December 9, 1909, June 11, 1900.

Morning Post, 21 May, 1931.

Evening News, 22 January, 1935.

Saturday Review, 14 May, 1904.

T.P.'s Weekly, April 27, 1929.

INDEX

INDEX